Rough Carpentry Illustrated

Elizabeth and Robert Williams

TAB BOOKS
Blue Ridge Summit, PA

FIRST EDITION
FIRST PRINTING

Library of Congress Cataloging-in-Publication Data

Williams, Elizabeth, 1942-
    Rough carpentry illustrated / by Elizabeth and Robert Williams.
      p. cm.
    Includes index.
    ISBN 0-8306-7435-7   ISBN 0-8306-3435-5
    1. Wooden-frame houses—Design and construction—Amateurs'
manuals. I. Williams, Robert Leonard, 1932- . II. Title.
TH4818.W6W55   1990
694'.2—dc20   90-40546
                                          CIP

TAB BOOKS offers software for sale. For information and a catalog,
please contact TAB Software Department, Blue Ridge Summit, PA 17294-0850.

Questions regarding the content of this book should be addressed to:

    Reader Inquiry Branch
    TAB BOOKS
    Blue Ridge Summit, PA 17294-0214

Acquisitions Editor: Kimberly Tabor
Book Editor: Cherie R. Blazer
Book Design: Jaclyn J. Boone
Cover Photograph: Brent Blair, Harrisburg, PA

Contents

Introduction

In this book the term "rough carpentry" will include all of the framing, the rafters, the roofing, and, in general, all of the wood construction that is invisible when the house is completed. By present standards, the rough carpenter should be able to complete all foundation wood work, subflooring, erection of wall frames; installation of roof rafters and floor and ceiling joists; roughing in of window and door openings; similar roughing in of stairways, basement steps, and disappearing stairs to attic; fireplace or flue openings; porches, decks, or patios; and all cross bracing and similar support work.

So many people want and need to save money on home construction. They need and want to know as much as possible about basic construction skills. It is toward these do-it-yourself enthusiasts who have the time, energy, motivation, and necessary skills to build their own homes or add to existing structures that this book is directed. Such ambitious workers might be young married couples wanting their own first home, retired couples who want a small retirement cottage or second home, or persons with limited or fixed incomes who wish to save money by doing as much of their own construction work as they can.

Age is only a small factor, if the individual is in sufficiently good health to drive a nail, saw a board, or lift a rafter and fasten it in place. Youngsters still in grade school can help with a great deal of the work described in these pages. Senior citizens similarly can do virtually all of the work, if they are in reasonably good health. Several years ago, a 90-year-old woman in South Carolina built most of her house.

If age is not necessarily a problem, neither is sex. Women have, over the years, demonstrated that they are highly competent in construction work. Any task described in this book can be done and done well by women who are serious about their work.

Neither is income a highly significant factor. Not everyone who wants to build his own house is on the low end of the wage scale. First of all, the question of whether you can afford to hire someone to build you a house is not as important as how well you want the work to be done. While professional carpenters are, as a rule, skilled and conscientious people, common sense tells us that strangers are not as concerned as the homeowner about saving money, conserving building materials, or taking that extra step to guarantee that the work is done to your own high standards.

Many people enjoy construction work, particularly on new structures and with new materials. The work is clean, healthful, safe, and very rewarding. There is great pleasure in watching your own house taking shape under your hands.

Therefore, this book encompasses the needs of all people—young and old, male and female, high and low income, busy or with time to spare—who want to roll up their sleeves and start to work on what is generally the largest investment the typical person ever makes: a house.

You do not have to be a skilled carpenter to do the necessary work on your new house. Every year thousands of total amateurs buy tools and plans and learn by trial and error the best and the worst ways to do carpentry work. Unfortunately, the error method can be costly in terms of time and money, so one of the purposes of this book is to provide a guide for the beginner who feels the need for guidance and suggestions.

This book provides detailed information on the basic carpentry methods. It is a comprehensive and practical approach to any ambitious do-it-yourself enthusiast who wants clear, basic, accessible instructions on all major facets of rough carpentry. Efforts have been made to keep the language in layman's terms.

The book begins with the foundation of the house and proceeds logically through the framing, all the way through to the roof of the house. While it does not specifically deal with electrical wiring, plumbing, or masonry, it addresses all of the actual carpentry processes and, when necessary, laps over into the areas of masonry work.

Unlike many books on carpentry topics, this one includes special material of interest to persons working alone. Many elements of building are easier if two or three persons are on the job, so that one can help lift and hold while another nails. When only one person is working, the job becomes increasingly difficult or troublesome at times. This book offers several helpful suggestions for solo workers, as well as a number of simple, easy-to-complete, and extremely helpful devices that single workers can make themselves.

As one example, there is a rafter spacer device that can save considerable time and frustration. It is rather difficult for one man to climb a ladder, mark a rafter junction with the ridgepole, climb back down and saw the rafter slant, then climb the ladder again to nail the rafter end in place. After this, the carpenter must again climb down the ladder and repeat the process for each rafter. The rafter spacer shows how the carpenter can cut all of his rafter slants, hold them in place, and nail them—without excessive loss of time and energy caused by repeated descents from the ladder. When the rafters are to be nailed to the top plate of the exterior wall, the rafter spacer can be used again to hold the rafter ends in perfect and stable position as they are nailed.

This book does not assume that each person who reads it will attempt to build a house. If you want to add a porch, or re-floor an old one, you can learn how this can be effectively accomplished. Or you can use the suggestions included here for adding a spare room to the house, or for building a carport or garage.

One very important element of this book is the prevention of decay and insect damage. One of the most frequent and costly mistakes made by the beginning carpenter is carelessness concerning the amount of moisture in the wood that is installed in a structure. Not only does moisture-laden wood tend to bend, sag, or curve under pressure, but the shrinking wood will allow nails to pull free, and the moisture attracts wood-eating insects.

You will be told of a number of necessary tools for the job, and you will also be alerted about unnecessary expenses for tools that are rarely used. Comments on care of tools are also included.

Throughout this book are warnings of the importance of measuring and cutting and nailing carefully. Please keep in mind that these comments are included for a specific and very important purpose. When a stud is nailed at an incorrect angle, there will be problems later when you attempt to nail up or install wall coverings. When door or window openings are not cut and measured precisely, there will be either tight fits that will not permit the window or door to close properly, or there will be loose windows and doors that permit loss of heating and cooling as well as an entrance for insects.

The topic of building permits is also discussed. These permits are a source of irritation to some people, but they are legal requirements of your town, county, or state and you can face severe penalties and considerable expense and inconvenience if you do not secure the permits.

While rough carpentry is not an excessively demanding job in the physical sense, there are various health hazards connected with the job that you must watch out for. These are discussed in detail. These warnings are not meant to be discouragements; they are simply intended to advise you for your own protection. You have not saved money if you must pay a doctor's bill as a result of an accident.

While this book is written in straightforward language whenever possible, there will be times when technical terms cannot be avoided. When such terms are used, they are defined immediately and explained as fully as necessary. There is also an extensive glossary containing a listing of terms that might be unfamiliar to the reader and worker. A detailed index is also included for fast location of needed materials.

You will find that do-it-yourself work can be rewarding and satisfying from several viewpoints. You will also be surprised at the skills you develop rapidly as work gets underway. Do not let mistakes of enthusiasm and inexperience cause you to doubt your abilities in the early stages of your work.

Do not let the idea of rough carpentry suggest to you that the work is not important. It is crucially important work that will become the basis of all the other work done on your project, and when it is done well, you can rest assured that your house or spare room or garage will be capable of serving you well for years to come.

Chapter **1**

An approach to rough carpentry

By definition, carpentry is the art and profession of measuring, cutting, and joining timbers or lumber into preplanned structures. The carpenter historically did all of the "rough" work on the building: he assembled the foundation timbers, erected the framing, and completed the skeletal roofing work. The carpenter was far more concerned with the physical strength and endurance of the building than he was with the attractive appearance of it. In most cases his work was considered "invisible," because after the building was completed the carpenter's work was seldom, if ever, seen.

In past decades, the two most important persons working on a building, from a standpoint of strength and stability, were the mason and the carpenter. The mason or his aides dug the footings and filled these with 6 inches of sand and gravel and, when the materials were available, added several inches of concrete. After the concrete had set, the mason laid the stones, cement blocks, or bricks that served as the foundation of the entire building. When the foundation walls were completed, the mason's work was done.

The carpenter's work preceded and followed the work of the mason. The carpenter was expected to build the forms that were used for the foundation walls, if they were to be poured or filled with concrete. The carpenter also constructed any other forms that were to be used for concrete, such as footings for chimneys, retaining walls, or basement floors.

After the mason had departed, the carpenter then went to work on the sleepers, or sills, of the frame of the house. The sleeper or sill is a huge timber, usually 2 × 6 or larger, standing upright and generally fastened at right angles to form the exterior limits of the house. After he had completed the entire skeletal structure of the house, the carpenter's work was done and the joiner's work began.

When the joiner arrived, he expected to find a framing that was stable, strong, rigid, and dependable, because the strength and endurance of the building depended upon the foundation walls and the framing. All load-bearing walls were the responsibility of the carpenter.

Any wall that supports the weight or part of the weight above it is considered a load-bearing wall. Any wall that does not support anything but its own weight is considered to be a partition wall. The load-bearing wall, if it is an exterior wall, supports in part the bracing, the rafters, roof sheathing, roof tiles or shingles, and insulation. It might, in buildings of more than one story, also support the upper floors of the building.

The partition wall may be constructed on any floor or even in the basement, and such walls may be removed, if desired, because they do not support any part of the building above them. They are used simply as decorative walls or as dividers to create two or more smaller rooms from one large room.

The work of the joiner, unlike that of the carpenter, was geared more toward convenience, beauty, comfort, and utility rather than toward strength and stability. The responsibility of the joiner, then, was to add the luxury, ornament, and geometric balance to the work of the carpenter.

In modern times, the work of the joiner and the rough carpenter have been united into one profession. A carpenter now does all of the work, from installing sills and joists to hanging doors and windows and installing arches, doors, and sometimes even cabinets and carpet. Today the only distinction made is between rough and finished carpentry, and the term "joiner" has slipped from the vocabulary of the house-building world.

WORK PLAN

Despite the name changes, the work remains basically the same in any type of carpentry. As indicated earlier, the carpenter will, at times, find that it is either convenient or necessary for him to work in mortar, metal, and several other materials, particularly if the worker is a do-it-yourself person who is working in his spare time and trying to save money or produce a better building project—or both.

We will take the amateur or relatively inexperienced worker from the lowest point of the building to the literal top of the building. The work begins underground—with the footings—and culminates at the roof. Much of the important work in the house or outbuilding, however, occurs between these two points.

Some attention will be given to the basic tools of the trade and the question of buying or renting, as well as tips on how to take care of equipment and to get the most for your money. You will also have to decide whether to work in a crew or alone, or, if conditions permit, to combine the two options.

You probably have more than a passing interest in saving money, and you will be given suggestions on how to save more money by buying carefully and by choosing your materials with economy in mind—being careful not to lap over into the area of false economy.

The first step is digging the footings. Although such work is not normally a part of rough carpentry, if you are faced with the question of digging your own footings or hiring the work done, you might find it worth your time and effort to do it yourself. After the footings and sills work have been completed, you will need to see that all sills, joists, and bracing work is done to your satisfaction, and at that point you will be directed in the completion of the subflooring.

In logical progression, the next step is the work on the wall framing, basement openings (if any), ceiling framing, window and door openings, and roof framing.

There is instruction on the installation of sheathing for the roof and, optionally, for floors as an underlay. While all houses or additions do not include stairways, there will be a segment of this book on construction of stairways and steps for those who need and plan to include them. Consideration will also be given to planning closet space and framing the closets, as well as to framing work on porches, decks, and carports.

WORKING ALONE OR IN A CREW?

Many people are fortunate enough to have plenty of neighbors or friends to help them with their work; others are lucky enough to have no one to help out. If this statement seems contradictory, consider that if you work with a crew, the work is not truly your own, while if you work alone, or with a spouse or family member, the work owes nothing to outsiders.

Working alone requires more time, more careful planning, and considerably more effort—particularly in the lifting processes—than does crew work. If you are paying the work crew, you can expect to dole out a minimum of $5−$12 per hour. If you have a crew of four, plus yourself, you will be paying $20 to $48 per hour, or $160 to $384 for an 8-hour day. Certainly the work will move much faster, but your costs will escalate alarmingly. Even if you pay only one helper $10 per hour, in one weekend you might have to pay out $250 for Friday afternoon, Saturday, and Sunday.

Your best bet, even if you are inexperienced, is to employ your spouse, son or daughter, or other family—whoever is available at little or no cost to you—and work slower, if necessary. However, there is no single universal answer to the question of whether to hire laborers. If you are living under cramped or other highly unacceptable conditions and must move to your own house as quickly as possible, then hiring workers might be the perfect answer for you.

Remember that when a crew member takes a break, for whatever reasons, his pay continues while his work stops. If you and the crew must wait for 2 hours for materials to be delivered, you are paying the workers for standing around and chatting. Similarly, if you start to work and bad weather forces you to curtail the day's activities, your crew members might expect to be paid, particularly if they forfeited other gainful employment in order to work for you.

Because saving money is one of the foremost attractions for do-it-yourself work—first try your hand at doing all of the work on your house or extra room if you can do so at all without suffering financially or physically. If you see that you simply cannot handle the work alone, then hire someone to help you on a part-time basis.

Many aspects of carpentry work are so simple that anyone with average strength and abilities can handle the work. Nailing down flooring or decking for a porch, for example, requires only the ability to place one board against another and then to sink nails through the board and into the joists or sills below. Putting up wood siding is equally simple, especially in the early stages. You can follow a few very simple instructions in order to get started, and afterwards you simply lap the bottom of the board to be nailed over the top of the previous siding board, then nail the top board in place. There are simple but very effective suggestions in Chapter 6 on how to cope with the minor demands of this part of your work.

One person working alone can, with some slight difficulty, install sills, sleepers, wall framing, and most of the other work involved in rough carpentry. You will probably need help when you are ready to install rafters or do other tasks in the roof framing work. Again, a spouse or other family member can help with most of this work.

If you are timid about your abilities, this feeling is very understandable. Remember, however, you will gain more and more confidence and skills as your work progresses.

OBTAINING TOOLS AND EQUIPMENT

One of the most frustrating facets of any kind of work is having to do it with inadequate or improper tools and equipment. In rough carpentry work you can invest a great deal of money, or you can operate on a tight budget and buy only what is totally necessary.

Consider the option of renting tools. Nearly every city of average size has some retail or rental store that will rent or lease the tools to you. The cost is nominal, but varies from one part of the country to another. However, if you purchase the bare necessities, you will not spend a great deal more than you would pay to rent the equipment, and you will have these tools to use again.

The basic equipment needed for rough carpentry include the following: a basic toolbox, a good-quality claw hammer, a power circular saw, a good pocketknife, a drill or brace-and-bit (sometimes called an auger), two sturdy screwdrivers (one with a slot head and one phillips head), a crow bar (often called a pry bar, wrecking bar, or construction bar), a level (the longer the better), a square, measuring tape or rule, a handsaw (particularly if you are working initially without electrical power), marking pencils, a medium-sized wood chisel, a punch, a plane, and a small sledge hammer or maul. Total cost of these tools—if you buy good quality merchandise—will run about $200, or slightly more.

The level of tool quality depends greatly on how much you expect to use the tools and how you plan to use them. Tools can be abused and damaged severely by improper use. A screwdriver is not a chisel and should not be used as one; a hammer should not be used where a crow bar is needed. Don't carelessly drop or throw your level aside when you are finished with it.

You can buy sufficient tools at most of the national store chains. Some of these stores charge a higher price but will replace any defective tools that break under reasonable usage. You will need to determine whether paying the higher price will be offset by the replacement of broken tools. You might find that it is more economical to buy a modestly priced tool and use it properly.

A pair of sawhorses is a necessity, but you can easily make them for $5 or less. One piece of equipment not totally necessary but a tremendous help is a 6-inch C clamp.

You can save considerable money by using a handsaw rather than a power saw, but you will lose a great deal of time. A cut that a power saw can make in 10 seconds may require 2 or 3 minutes with a handsaw, and the difference in energy expended is phenomenal. Remember, you will be cutting literally hundreds of pieces of lumber, unless you purchase the precut studding and unless you have planned your dimensions carefully enough that you can use standard lumber lengths.

If you are working with a crew, you will obviously need a hammer for each person. It is pointless to have paid workers standing idly while they wait for tools. Probably any workers you will hire will have their own tool kits, but if they do not have them, you will need to supply enough equipment that you get your money's worth from their work.

SUGGESTIONS FOR WORKING ALONE

If you elect to work alone, there are several suggestions that can speed up your work and make it more effective. There will be hundreds of times when you need someone to hold a length of lumber while you nail it or to help you lift a timber into position so that it can be nailed. If you are working alone, you will need to find ways that you can do the work of two or more men. You can use your ingenuity to figure out solutions to the majority of problems.

When you need to nail two timbers together at right angles and you find it virtually impossible to hold and nail at the same time, try this: Use two scraps of wood, each about a foot long, and place them about midway along the length of each timber, even with the bottom of the timber and at right angles to it. Then, sink a medium-sized nail through the timber and into the end of the scrap lumber on both sides of the timber and a foot apart (FIG. 1-1). When you are finished, the timber will stand alone and you can nail it in place easily. If you need to have the corner perfectly square, sink one nail into the two ends so that the two timbers will stay in place, then use your square to determine the exact angle. You might need to tap the far end of one or both of the timbers to get the precise angle

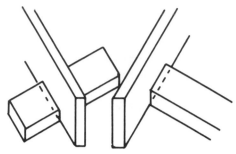

1-1 Join two lengths of timber by standing them in a stationary position temporarily and attaching short scraps of lumber to the sides of the timber.

you need. When both timbers are in place, find a length of scrap board or 2 × 4 and place the length across the top edges of the two timbers so that you form a triangle with the three units of lumber. You need to place the scrap length 2 or 3 feet from the point where the two timbers are joined (FIG. 1-2).

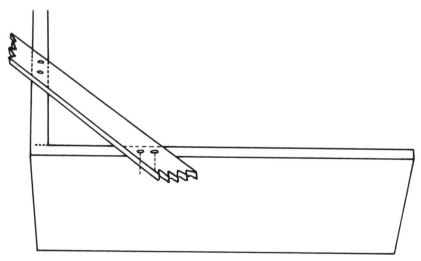

1-2 In order to maintain square corners while completing work on a project, nail a short length of scrap lumber across the corner formed by two boards.

Nail the scrap lumber in place by sinking a nail through the scrap length and into the top of each of the two timbers. Do not drive the nails in all the way, because you will need to remove them. The scrap lumber will now hold the two timbers perfectly in place and you can complete nailing the timbers together. When you are finished, remove the scrap lumber and save it for use at other locations.

Similar simple devices can be used in dozens of places to help you complete difficult steps in your work. When you are nailing up wood siding, one of the hardest tasks is to keep each succeeding piece of siding at the right lap. You will need to lap each piece 1 inch exactly, and it is often almost impossible to hold a 12-foot length of lumber in place and nail it while maintaining the proper 1-inch lap. If you are not very careful, one end will slip slightly, and soon the level line will be badly in error and very noticeable.

To keep such problems from occurring, use a chalk line and fasten one end at the end of the last piece of siding nailed in place. Carry the line to the other end of the piece of siding. The first end of the line should be fastened exactly 1 inch from the top of the piece, then you can pull the line tight and hold it 1 inch from the top at the other end. Snap the line and your lap line is established very clearly. You can tell immediately if you have lapped too much or too little.

If you don't have a chalk line you can accomplish the same effect by going to a point one-third of the length of the last siding board nailed in place and measure down 1 inch from the top edge of the board. Sink a small nail about 1/2 inch into the board.

Move now to a point two-thirds of the length of the siding board and sink another nail, just as you did earlier. When you are ready to nail the next piece, lift it and lay it upon the two nails. The board will be held exactly in place and you can nail it easily (FIG. 1-3).

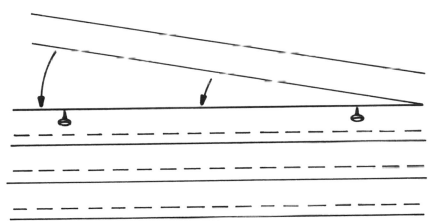

I-3   Rather than struggle with a length of siding in order to position and nail it accurately, drive a pair of nails into the siding piece already in place and lay the new piece atop the nails. The new piece of siding will be held solidly.

When you are nailing in joists, you will want the joists spaced exactly. If you want them 2 feet apart, be certain that you maintain that spacing across the entire dimensions of your framework. It takes considerable effort to stop and measure the space between joists before nailing. Worse than the expenditure of energy is the possibility that you will misread the tape or ruler or accidentally move the end of the joist. The result will be a joist that is improperly spaced, and if you do not catch your mistake, every joist from that point will be spaced incorrectly.

To prevent this, when you have measured and nailed in place the first two joists, carefully measure the space between the two joists. Measure at each end and in the center. The distance should be exactly the same at all points. Now find a scrap of 2-×-6 lumber and mark on it the distance between the joists. That distance, if you are spacing 2 feet on center, should be about 22 inches, but follow your own measurements in case your lumber has been finished to different dimensions. Finally, mark a 2-inch tongue in addition to the distance between joists and cut out the notches. You will be left with a T with a very thick stem.

This device will take you only a few minutes to make, and when you have finished, you have a guarantee that if you measured and cut carefully, and used the device properly, there is no way you can go astray in your joist spacing.

To use the spacer, simply place the tongue over the top edge of the last joist nailed in place and slide the stem of the T against the edge of the joist. Then slide the next joist in place so that the other tongue laps over the edge and the other edge of the T is against the joist. It takes only a second or two to position each new joist, and you can nail that end in place. Then walk to the other end and use the joist spacer again and nail those two ends. Repeat this process for each new joist. The work will move rapidly and accurately, and you will not have to worry that you measured wrong or that the joist was moved. You have only to use the spacer and nail.

If you have a partner helping you, make two of these spacers so that there will be one on each end of the joist. If you do not have a length of 2 × 6 you can spare, use a 1-×-5 board. It does not matter what you use as long as you can use it accurately.

You can use the same basic approach to make a rafter spacer when you are ready to frame your roof. You can also make a similar spacer for every section of your rough carpentry where you will need to nail in a number of pieces of lumber and have them spaced accurately.

If you are working alone and must hold a rather heavy piece of lumber in place and nail it while you hold it, here is a way to make the task somewhat easier: Determine where your nails must be placed in the piece you are lifting, then start the nails so that the points barely protrude through the lumber. When you hold the lumber in place your nails are ready and all you have to do is drive them into the second piece of wood.

When you are installing cross bridging bracing between joists, measure and mark your first pieces, then use these as a pattern and mark and cut several pieces at a time. This plan moves much faster than cutting one piece, stopping to install it, then cutting another piece. If you have used the joist spacer, all distances should be exactly the same and the cross bridging should fit all other locations.

All you need to worry about is that you use your first cut as a pattern. Do not use other cuts. Each time you mark a cut from a subsequent piece of bridging, you will gradually lengthen or even shorten the next cuts because your mark will be the width of one pencil mark off for each successive cut. In other words, when you mark and cut your first piece, you cut it to exact specifications. When you marked the second piece, you made the pencil mark beyond the length of the first piece. If you cut the second piece and then use it as a pattern for the third unit, your bracing will be one pencil mark longer on each end, and if you use the third piece as a pattern for the fourth, the length will continue to increase until you will find that you push the joists slightly apart in order to fit the bracing into the space. This means that your next joist space will be slightly wrong, and the error will be compounded for each succeeding brace.

This same problem holds true for all marking and cutting. Use the first piece as a pattern for all subsequent cuts. One other way to handle the problem is to cut off the pencil mark if you use different pieces for patterns. This means that your saw line should be just barely inside the pencil mark.

It might seem foolish to worry about a distance the width of a pencil mark, but this distance will become greater and greater until, after eight cuts, you have added 1/2 inch to the usual length.

When you are nailing in lumber overhead or in other difficult positions, use the C clamp to hold one end while you hold and nail the other. You can fit the clamp so that it includes the stationary lumber as well as the piece to be installed, and you can tighten the clamp only as much as needed so you do not scar or deface the lumber being installed (FIG. 1-4).

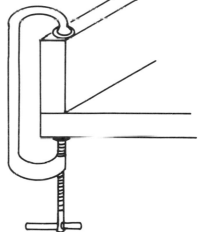

1-4   A C clamp is a very useful tool. Use it to hold timbers in place while nailing.

These are samples of how one person can, while working alone, handle some of the difficulties in rough carpentry. A number of other suggestions will be found throughout the book.

Under ordinary circumstances, all the work that you can do alone increases the amount of money that you save while you work. There are many areas of economy that will help you to realize even greater savings. Some of these are listed below.

SAVING TIME AND MONEY

In the first place, time often *is* money. Think about your carpentry project and consider your time carefully. If your project is some distance from your work or home and you must spend an hour on the road in order to work for an hour or two, you might want to re-evaluate your decision to rush to the work site and work for a couple of hours. The cost of operating an automobile to and from the site is money that must be considered in the cost of your building project. If the work site is very near your home or work place, then the practicality of working a short time is more obvious.

Consider the earning power of your time as compared to the savings of your work project. If you work on a commission, could you earn enough money in the time you would need to spend working on the project to enable you to pay professional carpenters to complete the work for you? For example, if an individual earns $250 an hour as a consultant, how wise or economical is it for him to dig his own footings? It might take the man 12 hours to do the work by hand, but a hired ditcher or trencher could perhaps do the work in 1 hour. This would save 11 hours, while 1 hour of the consultant's time would more than pay for the cost of renting the trencher or even hiring someone to do the work.

Also consider that every mile you drive your car, every minute of electrical power, and every minute you devote to an unnecessary task is money or its equivalent lost forever. You can save money by planning your trips to the supply house carefully. Organize your shopping schedule and list so that you do not have unnecessary trips to the lumber yard. It is better to overbuy than to have to make the extra trips, because most lumber dealers will agree to buy back from you any materials that are returned undamaged. Instead of buying only the precise number of 2 × 4s you think you will need, buy an extra 10 or 15. When the entire job is done, gather up all of the leftover materials and return these to the dealer for either a refund or credit against your bill.

If you do not have access to a truck, you might have to pay a delivery fee to have your supplies brought to your site. Do some telephone shopping to determine which firms will make free deliveries. Some charge as high as $35 for delivery, whether the merchandise consists of a full truckload or one board. Some firms waive the delivery fee if the total cost of the delivery is more than $200. If you are dealing with such a firm, it is far better to order a few more units of lumber and get free delivery than it is to pay a high delivery fee.

You will save money if you shop around for the best buys. One firm might be much cheaper on 2-×-6 lumber than is another firm. If you need a large number of these lumber units, it might pay you to buy that particular item from the dealer.

Some supply houses charge slightly more for precut studding than for regular 8-foot lengths of 2-×-4 lumber. A precut stud is slightly shorter than 8 feet, and you might be getting less lumber than you would get if you bought the 8-foot units. Remember, you will have to cut the 8-foot units to use them with sole plates and top plates in order to have a wall that is exactly 8 feet high.

An 8-foot wall is ideal in height, because Sheetrock, paneling, and other large units of building material come in 8-foot sections. If your wall is slightly higher than 8 feet, you will have difficulties, so buy the precut studding even if it is slightly more expensive. Otherwise, you will have to take the time to cut off 2 inches from each stud you install. This will cost you in time and energy, and the waste you cut off usually has no use whatever in building. You might find that precut studding is, in various stores, less expensive than 8-foot 2-x-4 lumber. If so, buy it for your studding.

One thing to remember about delivery fees is that if you order too far in advance to get the free delivery, you can have a great deal of expensive building material lying unguarded at the building site. You then run the risk of loss by theft, weather damage, vandalism, and breakage.

Examine the options. You might find that if you are building an entire house or if you have an extensive project under way, building supply houses will sometimes give you a contractor's price on everything you buy there. Ask for the special price. Do not be hesitant to inquire.

You can also save money by selecting your own lumber. In many lumber yards such practices are not permitted, but if your dealer has no objection, load your own lumber and reject any units that are defective. A 2-x-4 with a huge knot hole in it is useless as a stud, and if you buy it you are wasting money. As you move into larger units of lumber, costs rise sharply. Therefore, be certain that the 2 x 6 that is 16 feet long is perfectly sound before you accept it.

If the firm delivers your lumber to the site, lay aside all unacceptable lumber and return it for credit. Even if the dealer will not permit you to select your own lumber, you can usually watch the lumber being loaded. If you see a highly defective piece put on the truck, stop the loaders and tell them that you will not accept that one piece of lumber.

As you begin to work, you will have to cut off small sections of lumber from time to time. Lay these aside in a handy but out-of-the-way place. Then when you need a small scrap of lumber, you can get it from the pile rather than having to cut a sound unit of timber.

Inquire into the cost and coverage of construction insurance before you proceed very far with your work. Your budget might be severely damaged if you find to your dismay that someone stole a stack of materials while you were away from the job. Make it a practice to secure or lock up all tools and other easily removed items if you are going to be absent from the site for only a short time. Have delivered supplies placed in an unobtrusive location. Do not leave the materials in open view of anyone driving past the site. Temptation is often too great, particularly if there is no evidence of anyone around the work area.

Plan the use of larger units of lumber carefully. Try to plan so that 2-x-6 or larger lumber will not have to be cut if you need only a short length. Store materials not in use so they will not be damaged during the work.

Do not try so hard to save money that you fall into the false economy trap. If you place studs or joists too far apart, you will weaken the structure and render it more susceptible to damage from settling, shifting, and giving way under weight or wind pressure. Also, Sheetrock can be pulled loose or paneling separated from the walls. Molding can be damaged, and leaks can result from faulty roof construction.

Keep in mind that your work must be inspected, and you will be legally compelled to repair any substandard work so that it meets local requirements. Remember that the building code states the lowest level of acceptable construction; your own work should equal or exceed the building code at all points.

Plan your house dimensions intelligently in order to get maximum use from the supplies you purchase. You can also cut your work load greatly by planning better. Plan floor spans so that joists that are 12, 14, or 16 feet long can be used without cutting, and plan the length and width of the house in terms of feet numbers that will be divisible by 4. Otherwise, you will have to cut a sheet of paneling or Sheetrock, and there is seldom an efficient use for scraps of such materials.

Plan your porch or deck dimensions so that you do not have to cut off 1 foot of a 16-foot length of decking. This lumber is very expensive, and every time you install 16 boards, you have lost the equivalent of one entire unit of decking—not to mention the time and energy needed to cut the decking lumber, and the risk of a miscalculation that could render an entire length worthless or of limited value.

When you are ready to work, start with the basics of the house: the foundation and the framing. These are discussed in detail in the next chapter.

Chapter **2**

Foundation framing

Before you can do any work on the foundation and framing of your building, you must first be certain that your building plans will not vary from the building code of your town or county. In all cases in building, check with the local authorities before you undertake any project that will in any way alter the profile of your existing house or violate any regulations concerning new buildings.

CHECK BUILDING CODES

The building codes of any area might at times seem rather odd and even unfair, but generally the codes are for the welfare of all the people, and not some arbitrary standard set up for the purpose of creating difficulties.

Go to the courthouse, if you are uncertain about local permits and regulations. Secure a building permit. These permits usually cost very little and often are predicated upon the number of square feet in the building.

Also check on septic tank regulations and the feasibility of tapping into the city or county sewage system. In some areas the minimum size of the septic tank depends upon the number of bedrooms in the house, and the term "bedroom" is often defined as any room with a closet that could be used for sleeping quarters. This means that if you have plans for rooms with closets—even though you are not planning to use these rooms for sleeping—these rooms have the potential of serving as bedrooms, so the size of the septic tank must be larger and therefore costlier.

The argument behind the ruling is this: If, for example, a childless couple builds a house with four rooms with closets, then decides to sell the house to a family with six children, the rooms with closets would be converted into bedrooms. The septic tank currently in use would not be large enough to take care of the waste of eight people or more.

PRESERVE TOPSOIL

If you are doing all of the work on your house, including the excavation, now is the time to save the valuable topsoil, if your lot has it. This is usually the top 12 inches of dirt in any area and the richest and most desirable soil. If you have the lot excavated and all the dirt is hauled off, you will have to pay to have more topsoil hauled in before you can expect to have a lawn or trees or a garden that will flourish.

Instruct the bulldozer or earth mover operator to remove the top 12 inches of soil and pile it nearby but out of the way, so that later you can have it redistributed over your yard.

You do not need to have all of the topsoil removed. Remove only that part which will be under the house. Determine what the exact location of the house will be and stake off the corners. The excavation person can then remove the topsoil that is slightly larger than the boundaries as defined by the stakes.

If the topsoil is very sterile, you might as well have all of it hauled away. You can usually tell by a visual examination. If the soil is red dirt and if the weeds or grass growing there is stunted and thin, the soil is not likely to be very useful to you, particularly if it is extremely rocky in addition to being reddish.

Before you begin any excavation work, check with local offices for the possibility of buried fuel tanks, power lines, or telephone lines. It is entirely possible, unless you know the area well, that a house previously stood on the location and the oil tank remained underground when the house was demolished.

POURING THE FOOTINGS

If you choose not to excavate for a basement or to save the topsoil, you can proceed with the *footings*. These are trenches that outline the exact exterior walls of the house and are dug to a point below the frost line. In most parts of the nation this means digging at least 12 inches deep. If your soil is very loose or loamy, or if it is part of a previous farming terrace, you might have to dig much deeper. Dig until you strike deep red dirt that is sticky and almost like clay, if your part of the country has such soil. You might strike a layer of rock rather than red clay. If so, your footings are very likely to be sufficiently deep. You can dig the footings yourself with a shovel and pick or mattock, you can rent a trencher, or you can hire a professional.

Let your own economy, and spare time, physical condition, and even the weather determine how the footings are dug. If you are on a very tight budget and if the soil is loose, you can dig the footings yourself fairly easily, although you will need several hours or even days to complete the work. Working casually, you can dig 10 feet in an hour if the soil is easily workable. In one day you can have the footings completely dug, if the house you are building is small.

In extremely hot, dry weather and in soil that is very hard, digging time must be greatly extended. The hot weather will slow down your work and create health hazards. No matter how the footings are dug, they should follow exactly the exterior wall lines of the house. The house lines should be staked carefully and you should stop regularly to double check your progress for accuracy.

Once footings are dug, you can have them poured or you can do the work yourself. It is recommended that footings be 18 to 24 inches wide and deep enough to be below the frost line.

It is generally much easier to have footings poured than it is to do the work yourself. A typical cost of footings poured by concrete professionals is around $500. If you choose to do the work yourself, you will need a supply of sand and gravel, and you need to be in reasonably good physical condition before you attempt such hard work. Mixing concrete by hand is a very hard job, and you will need half an hour for each run of concrete you mix.

You can rent a mixer for about $20 to $25 per day, with a $25 deposit required. The job might require 2 or 3 days, so you will have about $75 tied up in rentals. Examine the economy of renting a mixer before you continue. Your total cost of mixer rental can be $100 or more if you are working alone and probably $50 minimum if you have help. Your concrete mix, sand, and gravel will cost at least $100. At this point you have at least $150 − $200 in rentals and materials, not considering any travel time, and you must still do the work yourself. If you must buy or rent a mortar box and then buy tools with which to work the mix, you will have about $300 invested. For another $200 you can have someone do the work for you.

You can use crude sand (from a stream or roadside) and save money on the cost of masonry sand. The pebbles in the crude sand will not interfere with the concrete mixture, although you would not want to use crude sand for mortar mixing. You can save $25 − $50 by providing your own sand.

When mixing your own, whether with rental mixer or by hand, you will find that you need a mixture of sand, cement, gravel, and water. Start by dumping 5 gallons of water into the mortar box (or into the mixer, if you rent one). Then add six heaping shovelfuls of sand. Mix the sand into the water and then add four more shovelfuls of sand. When this is mixed well, add the contents of a bag of concrete mix (portland cement). Mix this well with the sand and water and then add more sand until you have a total of 24 shovelfuls of sand for the entire mixture.

Do not be content merely to wet the sand. You must mix it fully and thoroughly into the concrete mixture. Keep the mixture fairly moist, adding enough water to keep the mixture plastic and workable. When the mixture is ready, add the gravel. If you used three shovelfuls of sand, you can add up to five shovelfuls of gravel to the mixture for each shovelful of sand used. Use a shovel and hoe for the best results, if you do not have access to a mixer.

Rake the hoe back and forth through the mixture until all of the sand has blended with the cement and water. Then when the gravel is added, do the same thing until all of the gravel is coated completely with cement. The sand is often referred to as the fine aggregate, and the gravel is called the coarse aggregate.

When the mix is ready, shovel part of it into a wheelbarrow and haul the concrete to your footing ditch. Start at one corner and dump in the mix. Use a trowel to smooth the concrete and level it. Use a long level to be sure that your footings are perfectly level.

As you haul additional concrete, continue smoothing and using the level until you have reached the corner of the house line. One way to insure a level footing is to drive stakes at various points along the trench and, by using a level laid atop a long 2 × 4, mark the points on the stakes where the level line should come. Use a thin paint line or felt tip pen line to show the correct level for the concrete.

When the footing is poured up to the level lines, remove the stakes and use the trowel to smooth the area where the stakes had been. You should now have one wall footing that is ready for use.

As you start the next wall footing, again use the level and the stakes so that the footings will be uniform. If you find that the level line is too low to the dirt, stop and dig out the trench until it is deep enough so that the footings are at least 6 inches deep.

A good practice is to shovel in 3 inches of sand and then add 3 inches of gravel on top of the sand before you start to pour concrete. Many builders, however, take a shortcut and omit the sand and gravel step.

Fill in the remainder of the footings, continuing to level and smooth as you work. If you find that you cannot pour all of the footings in one day, try to stop at the end of a wall. If you have a straight wall of concrete where you stop, the next day you will have a good wall to pour against.

Allow the footings to set or season for at least 24 hours before you start to lay concrete blocks for the foundation walls. If the weather is very cool and wet, you might want to allow an even longer time before you start laying blocks. Some builders will actually begin laying foundation wall blocks as soon as the concrete is poured, but unless you are in an extreme hurry, don't rush into the foundation work until the concrete is well set.

LAYING FOUNDATION BLOCK

When you are ready to lay blocks, use a mortar mix that is made like the concrete mix, except that you do not add the gravel or coarse aggregate. Your sand should be smooth and free of any pebbles or other foreign matter as you start to lay the blocks.

To lay blocks, use your trowel to spread a layer of mortar on top of the footings. The mortar should be thick enough to hold its shape when you cut through it with a trowel but it should not be dry. There should be enough moisture to allow you to spread the mortar as if it were hot oatmeal.

Before you start laying blocks, stake off the exact line for the exterior wall and stretch a cord between the stakes at a height of about 5 inches. The cord represents the outside wall line for the house. When you spread your mortar line, it should be wide enough for the block to rest on with an inch or so of mortar on each side of the block.

Push the block gently down into the mortar and use a short level to be sure that the block is level from side to side and from front to back.

Then check to see that the block is pulled so that it nearly touches the cord completely along the side of the block. The distance between block and cord should be the same at all points.

Next, "butter" the end of a block. Use the trowel to smear a generous helping of mortar on both corners of the block. Grasp the block by the thicker side of the middle partition and place your other hand on the end that is free of mortar. Gently place the block against the unbuttered

2-1 "Butter" blocks by applying mortar along the inner and outer edges of the blocks. Start at each corner of a wall and work toward the center, maintaining a good bond joint.

end of the previous block and push it firmly against the first block until the excess mortar is forced out between the two blocks (FIG. 2-1).

Now check the blocks to see that the second block is level from front to back and from side to side, and that the block is in proper position against the cord. Then check to see that the two blocks are level with each other.

Continue this process until you reach the end of the wall. At the end you might need to turn a block at a 90-degree angle to start the next wall line. This means that every other course or row of blocks will lap the one under it at each corner. Some masons like to build up corners at all four points to be sure that the corners will all be level. To do this, you will need to start at the corner with one block, then butt one against it, and work both directions until the topmost block is laid in that corner. This will leave a step effect on both walls.

Proceed like this for all four corners. Then stretch a cord along the bottom course of blocks. You can quickly fill in the space between the blocks by spreading mortar along the entire wall, then buttering and laying blocks until the space is filled.

Complete the second course by buttering the tops of the blocks in the first course and working as before. Continue until the entire space is filled, and proceed until the foundation wall on that side is completed. In the same manner, complete all other foundation walls.

WATERPROOFING AND REINFORCEMENT

Before you leave the concrete work, you might wish to buy and apply a waterproofing or sealing agent. You can use a paint brush or roller and apply the sealer like thick paint (FIG. 2-2). The sealer will prevent moisture from seeping through the underground portion of the foundation wall and into the crawl space of the house. Remember, moisture attracts termites, cockroaches, and other insects that can create damage, and they can be difficult to eradicate once they infest the house.

A procedure that can strengthen the house significantly is that of installing bolts, thread side up, in the foundation wall while the concrete or mortar is wet. You can fill the top blocks with concrete and embed the bolts every 10 or 12 feet along the wall line. Then you can drill holes in the sills and bolt the sills to the foundation wall. Such reinforcement will add greatly to the ability of the house to resist high winds and other tempestuous weather that would otherwise damage the house. The bolts are not an absolute necessity, but they are inexpensive and require very little time to install. If you use bolts, be sure to allow 3 inches of the bolt to stick up through the concrete.

BUILDING FRAMING PIERS

After the concrete work is done, you are ready to start on the piers for the framing. To build a pier, you may lay blocks or bricks after first digging a footing just as you did before, except that this time the footing will be only about 1 foot square. Dig down to the frost line again and fill in the

2-2 Sealing product applied with a paint roller. Seal all walls that will be underground.

bottom of the footing space with sand and then gravel before you pour the concrete. Lay blocks or bricks until the pier is up to the level of the foundation walls.

Piers should be located at the junction of all load-bearing walls and every 10 or 12 feet along unbroken wall lines, if there is no other type of permanent support.

When a pier is completed, double check its height by laying a long 2 × 4s or 2 × 6s from foundation wall to the top of the pier. Then lay a level on top of the timber. If the pier is not the proper height, make modifications at this point. You might need to use bricks or 1-inch solid concrete blocks to achieve the proper height.

INSTALLING SILLS

A *sill* is a heavy timber placed horizontally atop the foundation wall. The sill supports the headers and joists that are fastened to it at a later point.

To determine the location of the holes for the sills, save guesswork and physical work by using regular classroom chalk to coat the ends of the bolts. When all bolts on the wall are coated, lift the sill and place it carefully over the foundation wall in its exact position. Lower it until the bottom of the sill is in contact with the bolts. Try to hold the sill so that its outside edge is aligned with the foundation wall and so that the end of the

2-3 Drill holes in the sills that are large enough for the bolts to pass through. Push the threaded part of the bolt up from the bottom of the sill. You can also drill a larger hole to allow you to countersink the nuts on the bolts.

sill lines up with the outside corner of the wall. When you remove the sill, you will be able to see dots of chalk where the bolts touched the sill, and you can drill holes at this point (FIG. 2-3).

Drill the holes so that they are slightly larger than the bolts, just in case the alignment is not perfect. Lower the sill into place when holes are drilled and then tighten the nuts onto the bolts. The sill is thus anchored firmly to the foundation wall and you are ready to install headers.

If you are working alone and the sill proves to be too heavy or awkward for you to handle, here is a simple remedy for the problem: Drive a small nail through the sill about 1 inch from the end and in the center of the sill. Place a short section of 2-×-4 scrap over the nail. Tap the scrap lightly so that it is impaled on the nail sufficiently to stay in place as you lift the sill and place on end in position. The 2-×-4 scrap will keep the end of the sill from touching the ends of the bolts. Do this at both ends and you can move the sill and adjust it as you please until you have it in its exact position.

Use a claw hammer or crow bar and gently pull the nail out of one end of the sill. As the nail is drawn upward, so will the 2-×-4 scrap be pulled up until the ends of the bolts support the end of the sill. Repeat the process at the other end, and the sill will be resting completely on the ends of the bolts. Now that the sill has been chalked, you can drive the nails back into the sill. The force will cause the sill to be lifted above the bolt ends again, and you can lift the sill and drill the holes at the chalk marks.

If you are still uncertain that you have the exact alignment, nail two short lengths of 2-×-4 or 1-×-5 lumber to one side of the sill so that they can be turned down like a thumb latch. When the sill is in place over the bolts, turn the lengths of lumber so they point toward the ground. Slide the sill toward the inside of the house until the attached pieces of lumber are flush against the side of the foundation wall. If you wish, you can do the same at one end of the sill as well, so that you are guaranteed perfect alignment at the corner and on the side of the foundation wall.

Complete the process of withdrawing the nails until the underside of the sill is chalked, and you are ready to drill the holes. At this point you can remove the sills and nail the headers to the sills.

Nailing the headers

A *header* is a 2-×-6 or similar size timber that, installed, stands on end along the outer edge of the foundation wall. You cannot nail the headers in place while the sills are in position, because you need to sink the nails through the bottom of the sill and into the bottom edge of the header (FIG. 2-4).

With the sills removed, stand a header timber on edge and nail the sill to it. Use 20-penny nails spaced 1.5 feet apart along the entire length of the sill. When the two units are nailed together, you can replace the sill over the bolts, then add the nuts and tighten them thoroughly.

Do the same with the remaining sills and headers until the entire foundation wall of the house has sills and headers ready. If you have diffi-

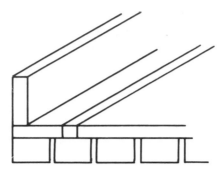

2-4 In foundation framing, the header is a heavy timber stood on edge so that joists or other timbers can be nailed to it.

culty holding the headers in place while you nail them to the sills, you can stand the header against two or three cement blocks. Then lean the sill against the same blocks so that the sill and header are at right angles and held steady so that you can nail them.

When all sills and headers are in place, you will find that at corners the header ends will abut. Sink 20-penny nails through the end of one header and into the comparable end of the other header.

At this point, the headers should be level along the tops and also perfectly vertical. If, for some reason, one or more of the headers are not vertical, straighten the timber before you install the double framing—if you choose to go to this extra expense and effort.

DOUBLE FRAMING

Double framing consists of adding a second 2 × 6 to the one that was nailed to the sill. The advantage of double framing is that you have the equivalent of a 4-×-6 rather than a 2-×-6 header completely outlining the foundation wall. Such reinforcements will provide greater support for the weight of the house. However, many builders believe that there is no real reason to go to this extra trouble and expense.

If you decide to double-frame, simply stand the second header against the first so that there is an overlapping of headers. One easy way to handle this is by cutting one header in half and starting in one corner with the half section. Nail it to the existing header, then go to full-length headers for the rest of the way. This will tie the headers together all around the perimeter of the house. You will finish the job with the odd half of the header you cut.

INSTALLING JOISTS

A *joist* is a parallel beam that holds up the floor of a building. A series of joists form a framework that supports the floor of any framed structure. The length of the joists and the frequency of placement of the joists depend, in part, on the length of the span of the house, and on what type load-bearing walls will be constructed over the floors (FIG. 2-5).

2-5 Joists actually support the floor and the weight of all of the interior of the house. To keep joists from turning, use cross bridging (shown at far end) or metal strips (in foregound). For maximum protection, use both.

Joists, which vary in size from 2 × 4 to 3 × 10, are usually 2 × 10 for ordinary frame building. For the best floor support, you should space joists 16 inches apart, although many fine professional carpenters use techniques employing joists that are anywhere from 16 inches to 4 feet apart, depending on size of joists and thicknesses of flooring materials. You need also to check your local county or city building code in order to utilize specifications set forth by officials.

When deciding how many joists you will need, mark your outside framing headers at each point a joist will be nailed. With these markings you will know, after cutting the joists, exactly where to place each joist at each side of the structure. The job will proceed much faster.

With the measuring completed, you are ready to cut the full-length floor joists to proper size. If you have a distance between two outside walls that is too great for one joist to cover, you need to build a girder or sill on a pier to give support where an additional joist will have to be added. For added support, joists that cross a girder should be cut 8 inches longer in order to provide an additional lap.

Once you have the joists cut and ready to install, locate the correct positions of the joists on the proper headers. Place the joists perpendicular, or abut joists to the headers and nail them.

Nailing methods

There are two methods for nailing joists in place, and for maximum strength you can use both techniques in your carpentry. One method requires locating and abutting joists onto proper headers. Then 16-penny nails are driven through the headers and into the cut edges, or end grain, of the joists. A second method toenails the joists in place by driving a nail through the joist at an angle and having the nail enter the header last.

To join the ends of joists that cross an inside girder or sill, you have a choice of three methods, any of which will give a strong union of timbers. The first simple method is to lap the ends of the joists where they cross the girder and toenail the joists to the girder, which is supported by a pier. The girder can be any type of strong and solid wood assembly on which the joists can rest for additional support. In addition to toenailing the joists, you can also nail them to each other.

A second means of fastening joists is to use both a girder and a ledger plate. A ledger plate is simply a length of strong lumber that is attached to the side of the girder. The purpose of the ledger is to provide added support for the ends of the joists.

When you look at the overall construction of this facet of the house framing, you see that there is a footing under the pier, and the pier extends nearly to the height of the joist. On top of the pier is a length of large timber (the girder), and the ledger plate is nailed to the side of the girder. The sum total of the holding power and support power of this combination of structural elements should be totally sufficient to support the house in all respects.

Notching

When you cross the girder with the joists, you can notch the joist ends (for hanging joist construction) so that the end of each joist rests partially on the girder and partially on the ledger plate. Part of the reason for using such a device is that if the joist portion on the girder should weaken, you still have the ledger to support the joist. Another reason is that you will have two separate anchor points for the joist ends, and when the joist ends are nailed to each other, you have three supports for each end. These supports will keep the joists from separating or leaning as they receive the pressure from the weight of the house and the additional pressure from the settling action of the house.

One important note to remember is that you should never notch a joist end more than $1/3$ of its width. If you are using a 2-×-10 joist, do not notch more than 3 inches in the joist.

Look at it this way: a 2-×-4 joist will never be sufficient to hold the weight that is placed upon it. You need a 2×6 at the minimum, even for small utility rooms, and at least a 2×8 for the usual part of the house. A 2×10 offers a great deal more strength and support power. If you notch a 2-×-10 joist end so that only 2 inches are left atop the girder, you are, in essence, returning to a 2-×-4 joist, which is unacceptable (FIG. 2-6).

When you use a ledger plate, you receive the support strength of nearly all of the joist. The only slight drawback is that you must notch the joist end twice instead of once (FIG. 2-7)

Reinforcements

For extra strength along wall lines, some builders install double joists or headers. These are timbers that are installed parallel to and fastened to the original outside joists or headers. Some builders prefer to nail the inside timbers against the initial timbers, while others like to use separators or spacers every 4 feet. Either method works well.

Be sure that the inside timbers are well supported by the sills. If they are not, you need to build a pier against the wall so that the weight of the interior timber has a resting point. Otherwise there is no advantage in having the second timbers. When you install the inside timbers, do not let the end of the new timber come where the initial timber ended. For best results, the end of one timber should be at the midpoint of the one to which it is fastened.

If the nails used are long enough to reach through both timbers, nail from the outside in. Then bend the ends for extra holding power.

When the inside timbers are installed, pause in your work long enough to walk around the framework of the building and make a thorough visual inspection of the progress you have made thus far.

Checking your work

Make sure that all of the work meets your standards. Check to see if the sills are resting accurately on the foundation wall. If there has been shifting, this can usually be corrected by hitting the juncture of sill and header with a maul several times. Do not strike the wood with enormous force; use just enough power to move the sill a tiny fraction of an inch at a time. It is not likely that the shifting created more than an inch or so of discrepancy. Check to determine that all subflooring is nailed thoroughly. Be

2-6   Abut joist into the headers and fasten them securely. If a joist spans as much as 15 or 16 feet, 2-×-10 timbers must be used.

especially careful about corners, if you are using plywood rather than boards (FIG. 2-8).

One particularly common trouble spot is with the cross bridging or bracing between joists. Often workers will nail the top of the brace piece

2-7 The added 2 × 4 or ledger plate adds support both to the header and to the joists.

and then forget to crawl under the joists to nail the bottom. Unless both ends of braces are firmly nailed, the braces serve no purpose (FIG. 2-9).

Cut a piece of 2-×-4 or 1-×-4 board the exact length of the distance between joists. This length can vary, depending upon your decision on spacing. Test several points to see if the joists are remaining vertical.

Now is the time to make any corrections in this first phase of framing work. In a short time it will be too late, so if you locate any joists with an improper distance between them, the most likely cause is that the joists

2-8 Space joists properly so subflooring will fit over joists and leave room for the next panel to abut the previous one.

are not properly braced and are starting to turn or twist slightly under pressure. This movement will grow worse as more weight is added, so if you are at all concerned, add more bracing at this point. Cut the braces according to the original pattern and drive the brace, if it is slightly long, into the space and then nail it securely. If the brace is too long on one side

2-9 Use 2-×-6 timbers for good cross bridging.

of the joist, it will be too short on the other side, unless you realign the joist spacing.

Use a level to check the wall lines and floor area. If you find a location that is off level, you need to correct it at this time. You can do so by using a thin shim or wedge driven between the foundation wall and the sill, but you might have to loosen the nuts on the bolts before the wedge will be effective. Tighten the nut again once the discrepancy has been corrected.

If you locate a trouble spot in the center of the floor, try to find the cause of the problem. You can often locate the trouble by standing a long 2 × 4 or 2 × 6 on edge at several places along the floor space. If at any point there is a long expanse of space between the timber and the floor, the floor is incorrect at that point. If part of the timber lies flat but one end is not in contact with the floor, you have a problem that needs immediate attention.

To check that the floor is level, you can also stretch a chalk line from one wall to another, but do not snap the line. Check to see if the line is in contact with the floor all the way across the floor.

If you find a location that is too low, you can jack up the floor at the point of the error, then insert a thin piece of wood on top of the pier or girder to bring the floor level up slightly. Sometimes a short piece of paneling is sufficient; if the problem is acute, you might need to use a 1-×-4 board or a section of 5/8-inch plywood (FIG. 2-10).

2-10 Stand or lay a straight timber across a trouble spot to help determine where the problem lies. If necessary, add a shim under the plywood to bring it up to the proper level.

A worse problem is a floor that is too high at some point. In this case, you might need to rework the pier or thin the girder slightly. If the discrepancy is less than 1/2 inch, do not go to any extreme lengths in order to correct it.

Once you are satisfied that your framing to this point is correct, you are ready to begin framing the walls. This next step is immensely important, and you will need to measure and double check your work several times.

During the wall framing work, you will install sole plates, corner posts, studding, cripple studs, window and door framing, and all partition studs and room framing. This work will be among the most critical and expensive of the entire operation, so you must take great care and be sure the work is done to your total satisfaction.

Chapter **3**

Wall framing

*I*n this part of your work you will install the *sole plate* first. This is the 2-×-4 border that is nailed in place flat around the entire outside wall of the house. Sole plates are also nailed in place for every interior wall in the house. One of the important steps is to see that each room outlined by the sole plates is completely square. Another is to see that the sole plates are marked accurately for the location of studdings.

INSTALLING SOLE PLATE AND TOP PLATE

Start by selecting the straightest, longest, and soundest 2 × 4s. Lay them along the exterior wall edge until you have completely bordered the entire exterior wall area. Once the entire border is complete, lay a second 2 × 4 beside the first, until you have doubled the border. The first 2 × 4 will become the sole plate of the wall, and the second will become the top plate. The *top plate*, like the sole plate, is a long, sound, and straight 2 × 4 that will become the top of the wall frame. Mark the sole plate and top plate at the same time (FIG. 3-1).

This marking is critical, because you are determining where all studs will be installed in the exterior wall. If the studs are not installed correctly, you will encounter great difficulty when you start to nail up Sheetrock or other interior wall coverings.

To mark the sole plates, after the 2 × 4s are laid side by side all around the exterior wall boundary, first mark the location of the corner posts. These will consist of two 2 × 4s on one side of the corner—a total of 5-inches of wall space.

From the corner of the floor to the first common or regular stud, there should be a distance of 16 inches on center. This measurement is extremely important, because later when you are nailing up sheathing for the exterior walls, you will need to have the sheathing or plywood extend from the outside corner to the center of the first common stud. If your measurements are not accurate, you will have to remove and reinstall the studding, or you will have to cut the first panel of sheathing to come out with a perfect fit.

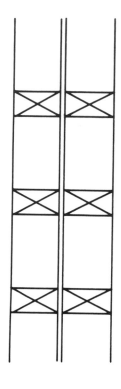

3-1 Lay the 2 × 4s that will serve as a top plate and sole plate side by side and mark them for stud locations.

Ideally, your wall measurements should be such that you will wind up with a full panel at the end of the wall, therefore odd-sized walls are a real handicap. If you are working from homemade plans, remember to have the total exterior wall length be a number divisible by four, if you want the studding and sheathing to fit without modification.

When you mark the sole plate and top plate, lay a square across both lengths of lumber and mark them both at the same time. This way you will make certain that there is no discrepancy in the locations of the studding. Remember that the first 2 × 4 you are marking will eventually become the sole plate, the timber on which the studs will rest after the timber is nailed to the subflooring. The top plate will cover the studding. If any of your marking is wrong, the studding will be oddly spaced or crooked.

You can mark the sole plate and top plate by using a square or by using a short length of 2 × 4 standing on edge. Mark on both sides of the 2 × 4, because the end of a stud will need to fit inside the marks you are making. The distance from the center of one mark to the center of the next should be exactly 16 inches. The only exception is at the corners: There should be 16 inches from the outside corner to the center of the first stud.

When you have completed marking, it is a good idea—especially if you are not an experienced carpenter—to construct the first stud wall. Turn the sole plate so that the 2 × 4 stands on edge and the markings are facing the outside of the house. Next, lay the top plate a little more than 8 feet away and parallel with the sole plate. Turn the top plate so that it stands on edge with the markings on the outside, or facing the interior of the house (FIG. 3-2).

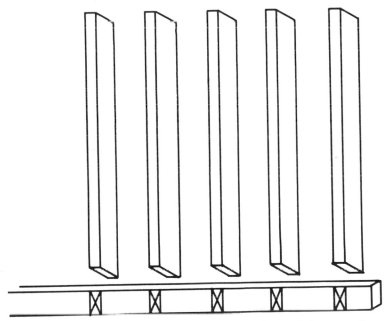

3-2 After plates are marked, spread the plates and lay the studs between them. Nail through the plates and into the ends of the studs.

Now place the studs at the proper locations. They should be placed so that you can nail up through the bottom of the sole plate and into the ends of the studs, and so you can also nail down through the top of the top plate and into the other ends of the studs.

You do not yet have your corner posts constructed, so you cannot complete the framing of the wall, but you can lay out the wall as you want it to become a permanent part of the house. When all the studs are laid out, you can move the top plate so that all of the components of the wall frame are in position to be nailed.

CONSTRUCTING DOOR FRAMES

Consult your plans to determine exactly where your door openings will be located. When you have done so, you can construct the door headers. The *header* is made up of two lengths of timber and spacers. You can use 2-×-4 or 2-×-6 lumber for the header itself and short lengths (the same at the width of the lumber you are using for headers) of 1-inch boards or plywood 4 inches wide as spacers.

Before you construct the header, you will need to build the rough door opening, if there is to be a door in the wall you are framing. The rough opening is the space in which the door, its framing, the header, and trimmers will be installed.

The opening itself is usually $2^1/2$ inches wider and $2^1/2$ inches higher than the door itself. You might want to add a fraction of an inch to be certain the space is wide enough. If your door is 32 inches wide and 80 inches high, you will need a rough opening that is $34^1/2$ inches wide and $82^1/2$ inches high.

Measure the distance between the studs on each side of the rough opening. Your headers will need to be that exact length. Cut the 2-×-4 or 2-×-6 lumber accordingly and then cut the spacers—the 1-inch board or plywood sections to use between the timbers. Lay one timber flat and place one spacer flush with the end of the timber. Another spacer should be placed at the halfway point, and a third placed flush with the other end.

Lay the second timber on top of the spacers so that it is aligned perfectly with the bottom timber. Drive nails through the top timber, the spacer, and into the bottom timber. Do the same at the other end and in the center. Use three nails at each location. You can use 16-penny nails for this purpose (FIG. 3-3).

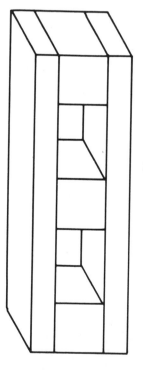

3-3 To make a header, sandwich three shorter blocks of wood between two long sections. Use 2-×-4 or 2-×-6 timber for this particular unit of construction.

Now stand the construction on end and lay a third piece of 2 × 4 (the same length) and nail this so that it closes in the header on that one end. You have completed the header and it can be installed between the studding for the rough door opening.

One easy way to install the header is to cut the trimmer studs for the inside of the door opening and nail these in place. The trimmer studs should be the length of the common studs, less the height of the header. If your header is 5^1/2 inches high (in actual height, not the nominal size of the lumber), then deduct that distance from the length of the trimmer studs. Remember that a 2 × 4 or 2 × 6 will not be exactly 2 × 4 inches or 2 × 6 inches. The stated or nominal dimensions are the sizes of the lumber when it is rough cut, not the finished size.

Measure, cut, and nail in both trimmer studs. Use 16-penny nails spaced 1 foot apart and staggered, so that the first is near the left edge of the trimmer stud and the second is near the right edge of the trimmer stud. Continue in this manner until you reach the top of the stud. Put two nails in the top and bottom of the trimmer for secure holding.

When both trimmer studs are installed, nail in the header by placing it so that the bottom rests against the top ends of the trimmer studs. Toe-nail through the header and into the studding, or nail through the studding and into the ends of the header. For added strength, you can use both types of nailing (FIG. 3-4).

If you are planning to lift the entire wall assembly alone, you will need to omit as much weight as possible, so you might leave the rough

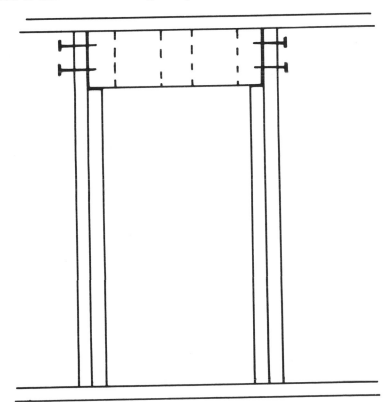

3-4 When installing a header, set it upon the top ends of trimmer studs and nail through the common stud and into the ends of the headers.

door framing without the trimmers and headers. If you will have help in lifting the wall frame, you can go ahead and install trimmers and headers.

When the header is in place, the door frame is complete and you are ready to move on to rough window openings.

COMPLETING ROUGH WINDOW OPENINGS

Your first step in framing the window opening is to build another header. The window header is constructed in almost the same manner as the door header. Measure the distance between the studding where you plan to locate the window and make sure that you are allowing enough space for the width of the window as well as the trimmers.

For the average window, a 4-foot-long header is usually about the right width. Measure your own to double-check on the space limitations.

The purpose of the window header (and the door header) is to provide as much support and strength as possible for the wall. It is somewhat surprising to many beginning builders to realize that the window area represents the greatest expanse of unsupported space in the entire house frame. This is especially true of the wide picture windows. Therefore, the header is a vitally important part of the wall frame.

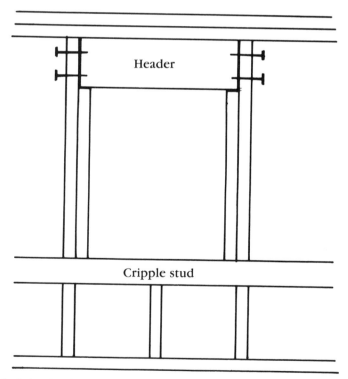

3-5 Install window headers in much the same fashion as door headers. Trimmer studs can be used so that the header will have a solid support on which to rest.

You can use 2-×-6 lumber for the window header, which is built just as you built the door header. Lay one length of the 2-×-6 lumber flat, add the spacers at each end and in the center, and lay another length of 2-×-4 lumber on top of the spacers. Nail these together as you did before (FIG. 3-5). The major differences are that you will need to use cripple studs under the windows and that the trimmers are in two pieces. The two-piece trimmers allow for the placement of the rough sill for the window.

You could nail in the rough sill across the opening just under the location the window would be installed, but you would have only the 20-penny nails to support all of the weight above. If you use two-piece trimmers, the rough sill can rest on the ends of the bottom sections of the trimmers. This provides trimmer support plus the support of the nails. There will also be the cripple studs below (and above) the windows (FIG. 3-6).

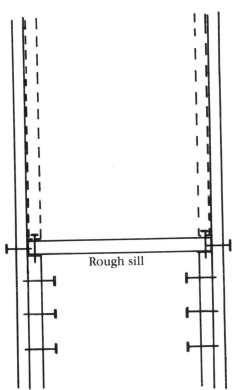

Rough sill

3-6 The rough sill can rest on the top ends of trimmer studs. Fasten the rough sill by driving nails through the top and into the ends of the trimmer studs, and by driving nails through the common studs and into the ends of the rough sill.

After you have determined the exact height of the window, measure and cut the rough sill, which can be a 2-×-4 length. Do not install the rough sill yet.

Measure and cut the bottom section of the trimmer studs and nail these to the existing studding. When these are in place, lay the rough sill so that the ends rest on the top ends of the bottom trimmers. Install the rough sill by driving nails through the studding and into the ends of the sill, and by driving nails down through the end of the sill and into the top ends of the bottom trimmers. Do this on both sides.

Nail in the window header so that the top of the header is even with the top of the studding. You can nail in the header as you did the door header, either by toenailing or by sinking nails through the stud and into the ends of the header units, or by doing both.

If the window is unusually short, install the header lower than the ends of the studs. If you do so, cut and install cripple studs above the window so that the shorter studs fit between the top plate and the top of the header. You will also need to measure and cut cripple studs to install between the bottom of the rough sill and the sole plate.

The usual pattern of installing cripples is to space and locate them as though an imaginary line ran through the rough window opening. The bottom cripples will be aligned with the top ones and they will be spaced like common studs.

MAKING CORNER AND PARTITION POSTS

You are not yet ready to erect your wall frame. The most important part of the wall is yet to come: the corner posts.

A *corner post* serves two extremely crucial functions. First, it must be strong enough to stabilize and support the corners of the wall frame. Two walls will meet here, and any weakness will be damaging to the entire structure. Second, the wall frame will be anchored to the corner post, so the post must be perfectly vertical and located so that the corner will be truly square.

The simplest way to construct a corner post is to use three 2 × 4s and shorter sections of a fourth. Start by cutting a regular 2 × 4 into three 18-inch sections. Sandwich these between two full-length studs (almost as you did when you constructed the headers). Then drive 20-penny nails through the top stud and the 18-inch section and into the bottom stud (FIG. 3-7).

The 18-inch sections should be located at either end of the studs and in the center. When you have completed nailing the units together, turn the unit so that the studs stand on edge and place a third 2 × 4 wide side down on the studs. Center the third stud and nail it in place (FIG. 3-8).

There are several other methods of making a corner post, but this one works well and is easily constructed. You can now start work on any partition posts you will need.

A *partition post* is installed wherever two walls will join in the house framework. Use the partition post, also called a partition stud, even if a common stud is installed only inches away. The purpose of the partition stud is to provide a good nailing point where a second wall abuts the regular frame.

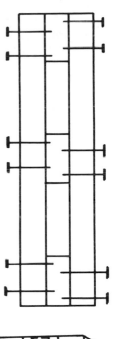

3-7 To make a corner post, sandwich three short lengths of 2 × 4 between two full-length studs. Then add a third 2 × 4 that lies over the center sections and covers half of the edges of the full-length 2 × 4s.

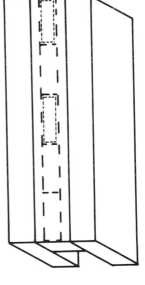

3-8 Add the third 2 × 4 while the first assembly is standing on the edges of the full-length 2 × 4s. The space on each side of the final 2 × 4 is used for a nailing surface later.

You can make a partition post almost as you make the corner post. Use two regular 2 × 4s and three more 18-inch sections of 2 × 4 lumber. Lay one stud flat and position the three sections of 2 × 4 so that one is flush with either end of the stud and the other is located in the center of the stud. Place the second common stud atop the three sections and nail the entire assembly together.

When you lay out the corner posts in the frame, position the post so that the 2 × 4 that was centered atop the two full-length studs is toward the interior of the room. Locate the partition stud or post so that the common studs are in the position of the regular studs. That is, have the post situated so that you can stand inside the house and see through the openings in the post. Measure carefully so that these posts align with the interior walls that will be erected later.

At this point all of the components of the entire wall frame assembly should be positioned as they will be placed in the wall frame when it is nailed in place. The sole plate is standing on edge, as is the top plate. The studs are all placed, on edge, within the framework and in their 16-inch on-center positions. The corner posts are laid out between top plate and sole plate, as are the partition posts where room walls will connect.

Now you can nail the entire assembly together. Use four nails in the top and bottom of the corner posts and partition studs. Use two nails in top and bottom of the common studs and cripples as well as trimmers. When the entire wall frame is nailed together, you need to check it carefully for squareness and trueness.

One method of checking is to have someone hold a tape measure at the bottom of the corner and pull the tape to the top corner of the other end of the frame. Write down the exact measurement. Then measure from the top of the corner to the bottom of the other end of the wall. Compare notes; the measurements should be exactly the same. If there is a fraction of an inch discrepancy, you do not have to worry, but if there is an inch or two, you need to double-check to see where the error occurred so that you can correct it before you raise the wall (FIG. 3-9).

You can also check by using a square on all four corners. They should all be square or very nearly so.

RAISING THE WALL FRAME

Once the wall frame is assembled and it checks out to your satisfaction, you can raise the frame. This is heavy work, and if you are working alone, you might experience considerable difficulty. Your safest bet is to hire someone to help you lift the wall, but if no one is available, there are some ways you can do the work without risking injury to your back or other parts of the body.

Working with helpers

First, if you have help, locate two lengths of 2 × 4 about a foot or so long (length is not a significant consideration). Nail these to the floor parallel to the top cap and at each end of the wall frame. Next, locate a long 1-×-5 or 2-×-4 board and nail it, using only one nail, near the top of the corner post. Nail a similar board to the final stud on the other end of the wall frame and near the top. Use only one nail in each unit of lumber.

You do not need to drive the nails all the way in at any of these points, and that includes the lengths of 2 × 4 you attached to the subflooring parallel to the top plate. These pieces of lumber will be removed as soon as the wall frame is erected.

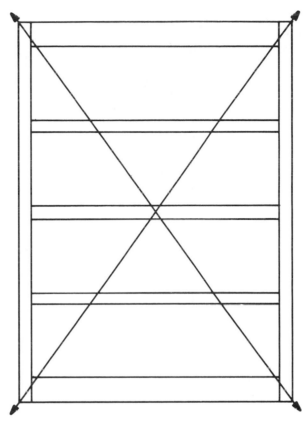

3-9 Measure a wall frame diagonally in both directions to be sure that the framing is square.

When the timbers are attached, have your crew lift the wall frame until it is erect. While it is held in place, have someone hold a level to the corner post. When the corner post is perfectly vertical, have a third person nail the attached timber to the length of 2 × 4 you nailed earlier to the subflooring.

On the other end of the wall frame, use the level again to see that the final stud is perfectly vertical. When it is ready, pull the second brace timber to the 2-×-4 section nailed to the subflooring near that end of the wall. Fasten the brace to the 2 × 4. At this time your wall frame should be vertical and ready to attach to the subflooring (FIG. 3-10).

Check the sole plate to be certain that it is perfectly parallel to the floor header at the outside edge of the wall. If it is not even with the edge, use a maul or heavy hammer and tap the sole plate until it moves into position. The brace running from the top of the wall frame to the 2-×-4 sections should not prevent your moving the sole plate slightly. You might have to tap the sole plate as much as 5 or 6 inches. Do not hit the sole plate hard; a gentle tapping will cause the wall frame to move slowly and gradually.

3-10 Use adequate bracing while the wall frames are being erected to avoid damage from high winds.

Begin the permanent locating of the wall frame by driving 20-penny nails through the sole plate between the studding and into the subflooring. Use at least two nails between every two studs, until you have covered the entire length of the wall frame. When the nailing is completed, do not remove the braces. At this point the wall frame is still very weak, and a high wind could easily blow the assembly down.

Your next step is to go to the next wall area and frame it just as you framed the first wall. When it is ready, raise it and anchor the braces and nail the sole plate to the floor, just as you did before.

Now you can pull the final stud of the second wall to the corner post and connect the two by nailing through the final stud and into the corner post. Space nails about 1 foot apart and use rows of two nails along the length of the stud.

At this point you have two wall frames erected and connected. Your wall assembly is now much stronger than it was, but do not remove the braces until you have connected the entire exterior wall frame. Do this by assembling the third wall and raising it and nailing the sole plate to the floor, as you did earlier, and by nailing the final stud to the corner post. When you have built and raised all four walls and all four are interconnected, you can remove the braces and the lengths of timber you nailed to the subflooring.

You will note that the sole plate continues unbroken all around the exterior walls of the house, even across doorways. Later, when you are ready to install doors, you can cut and remove the portion of sole plate under the doorways, but for now leave all of the sole plate intact.

Working Alone

If you are working alone and cannot secure help even for the time required to lift the wall frames, there are ways you can go about the work. One way is to build the wall into place. While this method is much slower and more difficult, it works.

Start by laying out your sole plate and marking it. This time you need to mark it on top rather than on the bottom. Mark the locations of the corner posts, partition studs, and common studs, as well as the locations of window and door frames. When the sole plate is marked, nail it in place, marked side up. Install the entire exterior dimension of the house in this fashion.

Assemble your corner posts. When they are ready, nail to the corner post a length of brace lumber, and nail to the floor a short piece of 2 × 4 near the sole plate and at right angles to it.

Before you lift the corner post into position atop the sole plate, have your hammer, nails, and a level ready. You will not be able to turn the corner post loose in order to get these tools.

Start two or three nails about 4 inches apart in the end of the brace piece that will soon be nailed to the corner post. While holding the corner post erect, push the end of the brace piece against the short length of lumber you nailed to the floor. While holding the level against the corner post with the other hand, slowly move the post, allowing the brace piece to slip easily through your hands as you do so, until the level shows you that the post is completely vertical. Hold the post steady while you move the brace slightly until one of the nails you started is in line with the corner post. When you are ready, tap the nail just enough for it to penetrate the corner post and hold. Lay the level and any other tools aside and drive the nail in until the brace is securely fastened to the post.

You will need to install a brace on the other wall side of the corner post, and you might have to make slight adjustments in the vertical position of the post. You have already done the hard part; the remainder is easily accomplished.

Now install the other corner post on the same wall. You will then have the complete sole plate and the corner posts ready. The next step is to install the partition posts or studs.

These studs are installed in much the same fashion as the corner posts. You will need one brace and anchor piece about 5 feet from the stud, toward the center of the floor, and another the same distance at right angles with the sole plate.

Proceed as you did before. Start nails in the brace piece, place one end against the anchor, and adjust the stud until it is vertical from that direction. Position the brace so that the nail is lined up with the post. Tap the nail until the brace will hold. Then repeat the steps with the brace from the other angle.

When you are satisfied that both corner posts and the partition studs or posts are placed properly, fasten these securely by toenailing through the posts and into the sole plate. It is a good idea to toenail on all four sides, using two nails per side. Use 20-penny nails for better holding power.

When all posts are secured and still perfectly vertical, you can install the top plate. Use a step ladder and do not lean it against the posts. If you do, they might be forced out of alignment or topple over.

Lay one end of a top plate, which should be a long, true, and sound 2 × 4, over the end of the corner post. Only an inch or two should be lapping over the far end of the post. Then lift the other end gently, and in a smooth motion, lay the plate on top of the junction or partition stud. Move to the corner post and lay the end over the post as well (FIG. 3-11).

If the top plate is not long enough to reach all the way to the corner post, measure the distance carefully from the outside edge of the corner post to the midpoint of the partition stud. Then measure and cut the top plate and lay it in place.

Any time you need to splice a timber, do it on top of a stud or partition post. The splice point will be the weakest part of the top plate and will need the firm support of the studding under it. If you must splice atop a common stud, you can install short support pieces under the top plate and nail to each side of the stud. These support pieces can be as short as 5 or 6 inches and should be of 2-×-4 timber.

Continue along the wall line until you have completed the installation of the top plate. You will notice that the plate tends to sag slightly, but this is not a matter for concern. When you add the studding, the plate will be solid and firm.

You are now ready to install studding. If you do not have precut studs, cut regular 2 × 4s the exact length of the corner post. These should also be the exact length of the partition post or stud. If you measure the distance from the bottom of the top plate to the top of the sole plate, you might find a very slight discrepancy because of the sagging of the top plate.

3-11   Arrange the ends of the top plate and top cap so they rest solidly on the support corner posts or partition posts.

Use the corner posts invariably. You can count the markings for stud placement and cut all the studs at one time. The length of the studs must be constant, so there should be no problem.

To install the studs, mark the top plate (on the top) as well as the sole plate. Wedge the stud between the two plates. If you need to do so, tap one or both ends of the stud until it is in perfect position. Nail the top first by driving nails through the top plate and down into the end of the stud. Then fasten the bottom end to the sole plate by toenailing the stud to the plate.

If you have trouble with the stud slipping or moving as you nail, make the work easier by following these steps: First, for the top plate nailing, you can cut a short length of 2 × 4 that is the exact length as the distance between the studs. Use the C clamp and fasten the stud spacer in place.

Now start the nail between the marking lines and drive it until it is seated well. With your free hand, push the stud firmly against the end of the spacer and hold it steadily there while you sink the first nail. Complete the nailing, then move to the bottom of the stud. Again place the spacer in position and toenail in the direction of the spacer. The force of the hammering will keep the stud from moving in the wrong direction. Once one side of the stud is nailed, you can tap the spacer free and toenail from the other side for added stability. Complete the installation of all common studs. You can now begin work on the rough window and door openings.

Window and door openings

Measure from the top of the sole plate to where the bottom of the rough sill will be. This distance may be anywhere from 2 feet to 3 or even 4 feet, depending upon the size of the windows.

Cut two trimmer studs and nail these to the inside of the studs, adjacent to the rough window opening. When this is done, you can install the rough sill and nail it to the top of the trimmer studs. Then nail through the adjacent stud and into the end of the rough sill.

Next, measure and cut the second half of the trimmer studs. First measure the distance from the top of the rough sill to the bottom of where the header will be installed. You might need to double-check the length of your windows. When you have marked and cut the trimmers, install these by nailing through the trimmer and into the adjacent stud.

At this point you can install the header by placing it in position atop the ends of the trimmer studs. Fasten the header in place by nailing through the back side of the adjacent stud and into the header timbers. Be sure you have fastened both of the timbers. You can also toenail through the header and into the adjacent studding on each side.

Install the cripple studs above and below the rough window opening. Measure the distance between the bottom of the rough sill and the top of the sole plate. Mark and cut the cripple studs and install them by toenailing the bottom end and by sinking nails through the rough sill and into the top of the cripple stud.

You can use the stud spacer for installing cripple studs also. For the cripple studs above the window opening, measure from the bottom of the top plate to the top of the header. When you have cut the cripples, install them by toenailing the bottom end to the top of the header and by driving nails down through the top of the top plate and into the end of the cripple stud.

Using the same procedures, install the trimmers and header for the rough door opening. You probably will not have to use any cripple studs above the door. Usually the door opening and the header will reach to the ceiling.

Before you leave the wall frame, use your square to check your work. First check the lower angle of the corner post and the sole plate. The angle should be perfectly square. Check also the angle at the top of the corner post and top plate. Use the stud spacer to check the distance between the studs. You should be able to place the spacer at the top of the studs and then lower the spacer slowly. It should barely fit at any and all points between the studs.

If you find an angle that is significantly incorrect, you need to correct it at this point. If all is correct, you are ready to begin bracing.

Bracing

There are several methods of bracing a wall. You particularly need to brace the corners, and one of the newer techniques is to use the steel braces. These are thin strips or bands of metal that run from the corner post across two or more studs and to the sole plate.

Many people prefer to use wood bracing, and this usually is either let-in bracing or cut-in bracing. Let-in bracing is done by cutting out a 1-inch-deep section from the studding. The cut-out is usually 4 inches long. Cut-in bracing is done by cutting lengths of 2 × 4s and installing these between the studding.

Let-in bracing To install let-in bracing, use a chalk line to mark the brace line from a point 5 feet high on the corner post to a point 6 feet away on the sole plate. Mark a second line parallel to the first and as far apart as the width of your bracing will be. If you use 4-inch boards, then the lines should be 4 inches apart.

When the lines are marked, use a hand saw to cut a slot an inch deep where each line crosses the studs. Then use a hammer and chisel to chip out the 4-inch section of wood. Do not chip out any wood from the sole plate or the corner post. Instead, when you are ready, hold the brace board in place so that it extends past the corner post and sole plate slightly. Mark the board against the sole plate and corner post and then saw the board at these points. You will have an angle cut on both ends of the board.

When the board is ready, hold it in its proper position and nail through the board and into the studding. Use two medium-sized nails at each stud. Where the board rests upon the sole plate and corner post, toe-nail from the outside and fasten the ends to the two points.

At this point you have firmly braced the corner on this one wall. Some people like to install another brace running from a point high on the studding to the bottom of the corner post, thereby providing double bracing for the corner. This type of bracing has its advantages but it also weakens the studding slightly (FIG. 3-12).

Cut-in bracing Cut-in bracing is altogether different. In this style of bracing you chalk your line from a point high on the corner post to the studding, as you did before. However, now you use 2 × 4s and cut the individual pieces to fit between the studs and between the final stud and the corner post.

When you have chalked your line, hold a length of 2 × 4 to the studding and align it with the chalk marks. Mark along the studs, on the inside, and cut the 2 × 4. It is good to start at the bottom and mark the first length so that the 2 × 4 fits neatly and snugly into the corner of the sole plate and stud. The second line will mark where the next stud and brace meet.

Cut the brace piece and install it by nailing down through the slant and into the sole plate. Do the same by nailing through the slant line at the other end and into the stud.

Repeat this process until you reach the corner post, at which point you will cut another slant line parallel with the corner post and nail it as you did to the sole plate. With all the brace lengths between these two

3-12 Let-in bracing.

points, maintain the straight line from corner post to sole plate. You will need to nail downward to fasten one end of the brace piece and upward to fasten the other end. Always use the slants for better nailing accessibility, but do not nail extremely close to the ends. You could split the wood and thus negate the holding power of the braces (FIG. 3-13).

3-13 Cut-in bracing.

Several times you have been advised to use short lengths of 2 × 4 or other timbers. Do not feel that you need to cut a full-length timber to get these short pieces. Use scraps that have been left over from previous cuts, if available. Use the same anchor pieces over and over. Save your scrap materials. They come in handy in a variety of places.

Solid bridging bracing A third type of bracing, which is not extremely effective as an only type of brace, but is a good addition to another bracing effort, is the solid bridging type of bracing. This type consists of lengths of 2 × 4s cut to fit horizontally between studding. Some people like to stagger the effect by using alternate heights of braces, with one brace one-third of the way from the bottom of the stud and another two-thirds of the way from the bottom. In the next stud space, one brace is used in the exact center of the stud.

Still other builders like to use two unbroken lines of braces across the entire wall, with one row of braces at the one-third point and the other at the two-thirds point. You can use the solid bridging along with the cut-in or let-in bracing.

Plywood bracing   A final type of bracing for corners is gaining favor and is now one of the most common types. It is highly effective and extremely easy to install. It consists simply of a sheet of plywood, 4 × 8 feet, installed on either side of the corner.

Plywood is incredibly strong, considering its thickness and weight. It is made from thin strips of wood in layers, with alternate layers crossing each other at right angles, and gains its strength from these crossed layers. The sheet of plywood resists warping from all directions.

To install plywood bracing, stand the panel alongside the corner post so that the outside edge of the corner post lines up perfectly with the outside edge of the plywood. The bottom edge of the plywood should rest upon the top of the foundation wall, and the top edge should reach the top of the top plate. The fourth edge should reach a point halfway across the second common stud. Be sure the lineup is accurate before you begin to nail.

Hold the plywood in position and drive nails through the plywood and into the corner post until the plywood will not slip or fall. Do not sink the nails all the way until you have checked the other locations for an accurate fit.

If all is correct, drive one nail through the plywood and into the top plate at the halfway point, and do the same with the sole plate. Now start 1 inch from the top of the panel where it fits over the stud and space nails 8 inches apart along the length of the stud. Do the same with all other edges of the plywood. When you have finished, that corner will be strong enough to resist high winds, warp, sag, and other problems that tend to destroy the squareness of a wall and later of a room.

When you complete the wall frame that connects with the wall you have just completed, install another panel of plywood so that the edge of the new panel will cover the edge of the first panel you installed. With two panels of plywood supporting the corner of the house, there will be little if any deviation from the position of the corner—except for a small amount of settling if the foundation wall and footings were not constructed adequately, or if the timbers were not adequately kiln-dried.

When you build the second wall frame, you will not use a second corner post where you have already installed one. Instead you will use a common stud. When the frame is ready to be lifted or when you construct the wall by using separate components, nail the end stud to the corner post and then add the bracing or plywood panels.

Continue constructing wall frames until you have completely finished the exterior framing of the house. If you have already constructed a frame on the floor and then find that you have to lift it yourself, below are some suggestions that might help you, particularly if the wall is a short one or if you are in good physical condition.

Lifting the wall

First, realize that the wall frame is very heavy and that you certainly take a chance on injuring your back or straining muscles or creating other physical damage to your body. If you choose to try to lift the wall, do not try to lift it into position without permitting yourself a chance to rest during the process.

The easiest way, short of using only brute strength, is to start by nailing two lengths of scrap lumber about 3 feet long to the end studs and to one stud in the center of the wall. Use only one nail and fasten the scrap lumber against a stud, using the inside of the studs on the ends of the wall or the insides of the corner posts. The scrap lumber should be about 4 inches or so from the top of the stud and you should be able to swing the scrap length downward when you are ready to do so.

Go to one corner and lift the corner of the wall frame until you can rest it against your knee. Hold it while you swing the first length of brace downward and let the corner rest upon it. The first corner is now about 3 feet high. Go to the center next and repeat the process. You will find that the center can be lifted much easier than the corner, now that you have a partial support.

Finally, you can lift the other corner and place the support brace in position. Now nail a long brace board to the top of the corner post or outside stud and allow the brace board to extend toward the opposite side of the house.

Nail a longer brace to the second stud on each end of the wall frame, and as you lift again, swing the longer braces into position. You will now have the wall frame 6 feet off the floor. The center of gravity has now shifted downward and the rest of the lift will be much easier.

Nail a floor brace piece about 10 feet from the wall, and line it up with the long brace board so that when you lift again the brace board will be dragged over the parallel brace. Lower the wall frame slightly so that the brace board will slip against the floor brace and hold the wall frame steady.

Repeat this process on the other corner, and your wall frame is now basically upright. You can start to nail the sole plate to the subflooring, and each nail you add will add strength to the wall's position. When you are ready, use the level and short brace timber to position the wall frame so that the corner post is perfectly vertical.

Proceed to nail both corner posts into position and complete nailing between the studding. The wall will be anchored securely at this point, but until it can be tied into the other wall frames, you will need to keep the wall braced.

Again, this method of erecting a wall frame is not easy and should not be attempted by anyone whose physical condition includes any problems with heart, back, muscles, or other conditions that would render the person susceptible to injury.

When all of the framing is completed, go back and add any bracing that is needed.

INSTALLING TOP CAPS

A top cap is a 2 × 4 that is added to the top plate and nailed to it. The top cap has two major functions: it ties the wall frame together and strengthens it, and it provides nailing spaces for ceiling rafters.

Start nailing in top caps by aligning one end of the cap with the outside edge of the top plate where it crosses the corner post.

The top cap will be long enough to reach to the point where the first partition wall will meet the exterior wall. At this point leave a space wide enough for a 2 × 4 to be nailed in place. When you later add the partition walls, the top cap of the new wall will be securely anchored to the exterior wall frame and thus provide greater strength and stability.

You will need to install the top caps completely around the entire exterior wall framing; always leave space for the other walls to be tied to it.

If you need to use shorter timbers, you can join them between studding or on top of studding, because there is already one thickness of 2-x-4 timber to support the roof and other weight that will be above the wall. Whenever you have an option, join the timbers above a stud.

When you reach corners, make certain that both top caps rest solidly on the corner post.

FRAMING INTERIOR WALLS

You can use a chalk line to indicate the wall lines of all interior walls. These walls include partition walls, closets, bathrooms, storage areas, and any and all other walls that will be covered when the interior of the house is finished.

As you chalk the lines, use two chalk marks to indicate the total width of the sole plates. Later, when you are nailing the sole plates to the floor, you will be able to tap the wall frame with a maul or sledge hammer until the sole plate is exactly in position.

Construct interior wall frames exactly as you did exterior wall frames. Start with the frames that will connect with the exterior wall frames. Lay out the sole plates and top plates and mark these for stud locations. Do not include corner posts, but do include partition studs or posts if other walls will later connect with the wall you are framing.

When the wall frames are completed, raise the frames and nail the sole plates to the floor. Nail the end studs to the partition studs or posts. Later you will top cap these walls as well and tie them into existing wall frames. Nail studs as securely as you would if the walls were exterior. Make no real distinctions between load-bearing and partition walls. All of the frame components should be considered important to the overall strength and efficiency of the finished structure.

As each wall is finished, make the chalk lines for the next wall and begin to construct the frame. As each succeeding frame is nailed in place and connected with other existing walls, the house frame becomes stronger and stronger.

There is no reason to use corner bracing or any of the cut-in or let-in bracing unless there will be particular stress placed on that wall. When you come to very small rooms (with walls of less than 5 feet—such as closets), you can nail the frame into place easily and without assistance. Here measurements and placement of the studs is still important, because you will need good nailing surfaces for paneling, gypsum board, or other types of wall coverings.

Be aware of the importance of interior doors and frame the rough door openings carefully. You will need to frame the rough door openings as carefully as you did those on the exterior wall frames.

Remember to check all corners. It is as difficult to install wall coverings in the interior rooms as it is on exterior walls. Be sure that all studs are still spaced 16 inches on center, and maintain squareness where floor and wall meet and where ceiling and wall meet.

If you have not planned ahead carefully, this is the time to make final decisions on plumbing and wiring. It is good planning to have two bathrooms on a single floor join back-to-back, to conserve on the cost of the plumbing. If you are planning to build one bathroom upstairs, or one in the basement, try to plan so that one bathroom can be built just above or under the other. Again, you save money on pipe and costs of plumbing.

Planning for ductwork for the heating and cooling system should be done by this time also. When the framing work is done, the time is right to make final changes, if any, in the manner electrical work will be finished. Nearly everyone wants the electrical outlets placed in the baseboard or within 1 foot of the floor. The reasoning is that drapes and furniture will hide the outlets. However, it is also difficult to reach under the coffee tables or lamp tables or behind chairs to connect and disconnect lamps or other small appliances, so you might want to do your own planning along these lines.

If you have a number of shorter lengths of 2-x-4 lumber left over from other cuts, you can cut braces from these partial timbers and install them for extra firmness and strength in the house. Do not install them gratuitously, but if you feel that the walls need extra strength—particularly exterior walls—this is a good time to install extra bracing.

When you have finished the top cap and subsequent work, you are ready to frame the ceilings. Here the work will move rapidly, but the work areas are often cramped and there is the constant danger of falling or dropping tools.

Chapter 4

Framing the ceiling

*O*ne of the major considerations you must face when framing the ceiling and installing the joists is that you will need very long, sound, and true timbers. The ceiling joists must reach from one wall to another and have sufficient length to allow the joists to cover the width of the top caps of the wall frames (FIG. 4-1).

A *ceiling joist* is any timber that connects the opposite walls of a room or building and that will eventually hold the ceiling and provide the framing for the attic flooring, if any. Because these joists—which might have to be 20 feet long or even longer—have to cover such a wide expanse, defective joists must not be used. It is also inadvisable to splice joists anywhere except on top of walls.

INSTALLING JOISTS

There are two basic ways to connect joists: butt-jointing or lap-jointing them.

Butt-jointed joists are those placed end to end, with each end fastened separately to the top plate or top cap (FIG. 4-2). A lap-jointed joist is one that is actually lapped, one end over the other, for 6 inches up to a foot. The two ends are nailed to each other and the combined lapped ends are then nailed to the top plate or top cap (FIG. 4-3).

Butt-jointed joists need extra strength, because these joists are largely responsible for the stability of the tops of the walls of the room or house. You have already seen how bottom portions of walls are braced by cut-in or let-in bracing or solid bridging. The tops of the walls, however, are seldom braced, other than through the use of panels of plywood.

Before joists are installed, check the stability of the walls. Hold a stud and pull back and forth at the bottom of the stud and again at the top. You will likely find that the top of the stud has far more flexibility than the bottom. When high winds strike the house, it is the top part of the wall and the materials connected to it that are most likely to be damaged.

The easiest way to provide the extra strength for the joists is to nail a length of 2 × 4 to the abutted joists so that the new length of timber will cover both ends of the joists. You can use a timber section from 2 to 3 feet

4-1 Building codes often require supports every 12 to 15 feet. Avoid long unsupported sections of floor.

in length to lap the joists, and you can use 16-penny nails to fasten the lap section (FIG. 4-4).

Before you install any ceiling joists, consider how steep the pitch of the roof will be. Remember that the slant of the roof will cause the roof

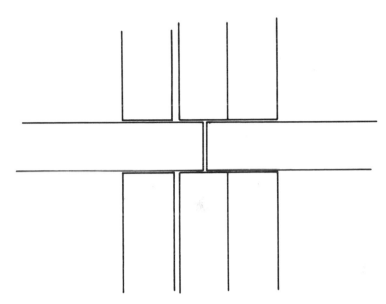

4-2 Often joists are butt-jointed atop a girder. To do so, abut the ends of the joists at the midpoint of the girder or plate and nail them in turn to the girder or plates.

rafters to descend past the ceiling joists. Unless the joist ends are slanted, the rafters can come into contact with the joists and cause the roof line to be aligned improperly.

If you plan to extend the joists past the wall line so that the joist ends become part of the framing for the eaves, your rafters will probably be fastened to the joists, thus making the slant of the joists crucial. This is the common way of framing the eaves and the way you will most likely plan to frame your ceiling.

Also decide the size timbers you will use for ceiling joists. Most builders use 2 × 4s, but for greater strength and stability many use 2-×-6 timbers. The 2 × 6s cost considerably more, but they are worth the extra expense (FIGS. 4-5 and 4-6).

If you are not certain how to slant the ends of ceiling joists, determine the height of the roof peak and then hold or nail a rafter temporarily in place so that you can mark the joist ends.

If the roof peak is to be 6 feet higher than the top of the ceiling joists, place a 2 × 4 in the exact center of the end wall and extend it until the top end is exactly 6 feet higher than the top of the joists. Mark a point 6 feet from the end of the 2 × 4 and line up the mark with the top of the ceiling joist. Drive one 16-penny nail into the 2 × 4, then use your level to check for vertical accuracy. Double-check the distance on each side of the 2 × 4 to the end of the wall frame as well. When the 2 × 4 is perfectly centered, add another nail to hold it stable (FIG. 4-7).

Lay a ceiling joist in place atop the outside wall frame next. Then climb back to the 2-×-4 peak piece and hold a roof rafter even with the top of the 2 × 4. Have someone mark the angle where the rafter crosses the joist end (FIG. 4-8).

4-3 Lap-jointed joist ends meet atop a girder or plate and are nailed to each other as well as to the girder or plate. For best results there should be at least a 12-inch lap.

If you are working alone, use the C clamp to hold the rafter in place at the top of the 2 × 4. Be sure to mark where the bottom of the rafter crosses the joist line.

You can also use a chalk line to achieve the same angle. Fasten one end of the chalk line securely and then pull the line very tight before you snap it to determine the rafter crossing line.

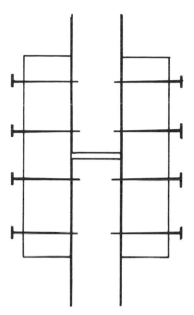

4-4   A simple way to strengthen butt-jointed joists is to nail a 2-foot timber section on each side of the point of jointing.

When the joist end is marked, you can cut the end at the proper slant. Use this joist as a pattern for all other joists you will use on that part of the house. You may now determine how many joists you will need. Cut the ends properly. You are now ready to nail the joists in place.

Space the joists as you did the studs, so that they are 16 inches apart on-center. If you decide later to add a plywood floor in the attic, you will need the exact spacing to provide the proper nailing surfaces for the plywood. Even if you add nothing in the attic but insulation, you will need the proper spacing. Insulation rolls are usually manufactured in widths that allow the worker to fill the space between joists exactly with one layer of insulation. If joists are spaced incorrectly, you will need to cut strips of insulation to pack in the extra space, or you will need to trim the regular insulation so that it will fit between the joists.

You can use the same section of timber that you used earlier when you installed studding. The stud spacer will also function as a joist spacer. If you want to make the work even easier, use the joist spacer that was suggested earlier. This spacer will allow you to space and hold the joist firmly in place while you nail. It will also speed up your work and decrease the effort.

After the first ceiling joist is installed on top of the exterior wall frame (so that the outside edge of the joist is flush upon the outside edge of the top cap), you can position the first cutout of the joist spacer over the top of the joist. Then move the next joist into the second cutout. You can toe-nail easily without having to worry about trying to hold the joist in place while you hammer.

4-5 Nail rafters and joists together where they meet at top plates or top caps.

4-6 Do not use rafters smaller than 2 × 6.

4-7 One method of framing a roof peak before rafters are added to the ridge timber.

For greater speed in installation, position your ladder so that you can install two joists without having to stop to move. If you are working from a scaffold, you can install six or eight joists without having to move.

FRAMING STAIRWAY OPENINGS

If you plan to have a stairway into the attic, you need to frame the opening as you install the joists. First determine the dimensions of the stairway,

4-8 Mark angle cuts carefully so that the ends of rafters will meet the ridge timber snugly and allow for solid nailing.

then double-frame the opening. See Chapter 2 for details on how to frame an opening in the subflooring.

The size of the stairway will mean that at least one joist must be cut, and where you cut the joist you should immediately install a header. Use 16-penny nails to fasten the header to the ends of the joists (FIG. 4-9).

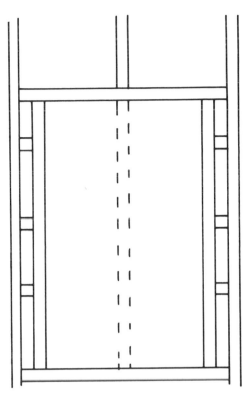

4-9   When cutting or removing a joist, frame in the stairway opening by using headers and short joist timbers, plus bracing.

There should be a header at each end of the opening, and if space will permit, double-frame the entire opening. If the opening is for a disappearing stairway, the framing of the opening should support the entire weight of persons using the stairs. The stairs themselves will be fastened to the framing, and there will be no support at all from the point where the stairs touch the floor to the framing itself.

For disappearing stairways, you will need an opening about 6 feet in length and 2 feet in width. In many houses the disappearing stairways are placed over other stairs in order to minimize lost space. The height involved means that extra care should be used in installation of the stairs.

When you install the first header and nail it to the ends of the ceiling joists, use three 20-penny nails at each connection, but do not nail near the edges of the timbers. These large nails are needed for strength and weight-bearing, but they can also cause splitting—which will negate the effect of the nails—if the nails are too near the edges of the wood.

When you double-frame the opening, use rows of three 20-penny or 16-penny nails if you are using 2-x-6 timbers. If you are using 2 × 4s, use rows of two nails. The rows should be a foot apart and each nail should be sunk fully to prevent pull-out and weakening.

The top of the stairs should be fastened in the center of the ceiling area so that climbers will rise into the tallest part of the attic. Where the head of the stairs is fastened, be sure to double-brace and use bolts rather than nails, if possible. If not, use nails that are at least 16-penny in size.

One method of strengthening the joists on each side of the stairway is to sandwich a length of plywood between the two pieces of the double bracing. As mentioned earlier, plywood is extremely strong and it will keep the joists from sagging or bending during usage. Even if the wood had not been cured completely and still contained an excessive amount of sap, the plywood will prevent warping or curving because the wood will slowly cure in the heat of the attic.

Regular stairway openings are framed in a similar manner. A major distinction is that stairways have thicker wood stringers and are therefore stronger than disappearing stairways. *Stringers* are the sides of the stairways that support the treads or steps, and are also called strings, horses, and carriages. Traditional stairs also have strong supports under them so that the weight is more evenly distributed. The *risers*—the wood that forms the back of the steps—in traditional stairs also adds to the strength of the stairs, while in disappearing stairways there are no risers in the traditional sense.

You will need more space for traditional stairs than you would for disappearing stairways. In the latter there are usually eight or nine steps, or treads, while in traditional stairs there may be 12 or 13 risers.

Disappearing stairways have steps that are, as a rule, 16 inches wide and 3 inches deep. The risers are, if present at all, usually 10 inches high. Traditional stairway treads are 3 feet wide, and the risers are often 10 inches high, like those of disappearing stairways. The treads of traditional stairways tend to be as deep as 1 foot, compared to the 3-inch depth of the disappearing counterparts.

While disappearing stairways require 6 feet of linear space for the entire ascent, traditional stairways regularly need as much as 10 feet, plus a landing. You will need to determine which type of stairs you plan to install, if any, and the steepness of the ascent of the traditional stairway.

FINISHING TOUCHES

Some builders like to include a valley structure in the ceiling work. This consists of a 2 × 6 running the length of the entire main structure from one exterior wall to the other. It is usually not one unbroken timber, but several timbers end-to-end, with another 2 × 6 nailed to the outside edge of the flat one and standing at right angles.

Valleys

The purpose of the valley is to provide a nailing base for all roof supports. The 2 × 6 is nailed to the top plate or top cap, and the upright section is nailed so that no two timbers end at the same place, except at the end of the valley.

If you choose to use this device, nail the first timbers into place, and when you install the upright timber, use a timber that is not the same length as the first one installed. If you do not have a timber of odd length, you might want to saw one in half and use the first half at the beginning of the installation point. This will mean that the first upright will end halfway down the length of the flat timber (FIG. 4-10).

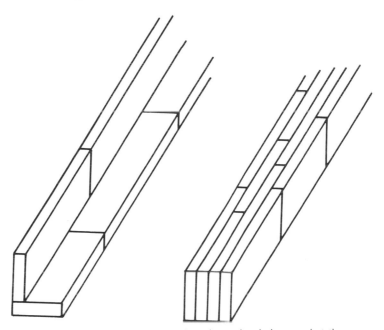

4-10 A valley. In this and in girder construction, do not let timbers end at the same point.

Next, use regular lengths of upright timbers and continue nailing these in place until you come to the end of the valley. Here you can use the final half of the timber that you cut when you began to install upright timbers.

The upright portion of the valley will now provide excellent nailing surfaces for the ridgepole timber supports. When you nail in these supports, toenail the bottom end of each support to the horizontal part of the valley. Then nail the upright portion of the roof support to the valley timber that is standing on edge. By doing so, you have provided additional stability for the roof supports.

When it is handy to do so, nail the upright piece of the valley to the edge of the horizontal timber. In this fashion you have the vertical timber standing on edge and resting upon the top plate of the ceiling, and the bottom edge nailed securely to the horizontal timber. Use 16-penny nails spaced a foot or so apart along the length of the horizontal and vertical timbers.

With the roof supports nailed securely, you don't have to worry that they will waver or shift in high winds. Roof braces, collars, and other supports will also be added later in the construction.

Bridging

Do not forget to install bridging between the ceiling joists before you leave this portion of your work. These joists are long and unsupported, and they can be shifted easily as you work. If they are misaligned by even an inch or so, your ceiling covering can be a difficult chore to install.

When installing bridging, be careful not to force the joists out of alignment. There is a general tendency among beginning builders to secure the tightest fits possible in bracing and bridging. If you cut the bridging timbers only 1/4 inch long, you will have to force the joists slightly apart in order to tap the bridging into position.

Assume that you cut the second bridging timber from the same pattern that was used for the first cut. Each succeeding timber, because of the added width of the pencil mark, will "grow" slightly longer, and the joists will be forced farther and farther apart. Within a matter of a few feet you can add more than an inch to the space between the joists. Not only will this added inch prove difficult in later ceiling covering installation, but you will find that the bridging timbers on the other side of the mis-aligned joist timber must be cut shorter than usual to be fitted into the space.

The best way to install the bridging is to cut a timber that will fit snugly but not tightly between the joists. Try this piece of bridging in several places to be sure that it will fit in a universal fashion. Then cut all of your bridging timbers from this one pattern.

When you find that the bridging timber will not fit between joists in a particular spot in the room, or when there is a space between joists and bridging, your problem is not the length of the bridging but in the milling of the joists. It is not at all unusual to find joist timbers (or other timbers) that come from the lumber yard in untrue cuts.

When joists are not cut straight, continue to use the bridging timbers just as you have cut them. Position the timbers between the joists and, if necessary, tap the end of the timber until you have forced it into its proper position.

If the bridging timber fits snugly so that it will be held in place by the pressure, you have a good fit. If you have to force the bridging timber too much, you need to check to see if you are also forcing the joist out of alignment with the rest of the framing. Your problem might be that the joist is not straight, or it might be that you have a bridging timber that is too long installed on the other side of the joist.

One way to check is to find a straight 2 × 4 and hold it against the joist, with the top edge of the 2 × 4 against the side of the joist. If the joist and 2 × 4 remain flush, the joist is straight in the area tested. You can also use a chalk line to make the test. Tap a nail in place at one end of the joist and then loop the chalk line over it so that it is snug against the joist. Go to the other end of the joist and pull the line tight. If the joist is crooked, the line will not touch at all points.

If you need to straighten a joist that has a crooked top edge, cut a strip of plywood and clamp it to the joist so that the two edges are flush. Bend the joist by using a pry bar, then nail the plywood in place. Do this along the entire length of the joist, and the plywood will hold the joist straight. Stand the joist on edge and push down with your weight until the joist bends slightly—enough so that the edge of the joist and that of the plywood are flush. Then nail the two together by placing two nails every 2 or 3 feet.

One test of a timber is its weight. Lift a 2 × 4 that is new, then lift a well-cured one. If you can readily detect a significant difference between the weights of the two, you have probably bought a partially cured 2 × 4.

Ideally cured lumber has more than 80 percent of the moisture removed from it. Any time there is more than 20 percent sap or other moisture in lumber, the wood provides a superb breeding and feeding place for termites and other wood-damaging insects.

One distinction should be made: If you are using timbers that have been treated against decay and water damage, these will weigh more than a normally cured timber.

When you are installing ceiling joists it is a good idea to butt-joint them over a wall frame and continue the same line of joists across the entire house. You strengthen not only the joist locations but the walls themselves when you do so. You also make it easy to maintain an accurate spacing of joists for later ease in installing ceilings or subflooring.

If you lap-joint the joists, you must remember to make the lap in the same direction each time. That is, if you lap the first joist on your left as you face the lap, make sure that all other laps are to your left as you face the same way. If not, you will later discover that some of your joists are 4 inches off in the center-to-center measurements.

When you are ready to install subflooring or other covering over the joists, if you find that your joists, because of lap-joining, are off center, make the adjustment in the space nearest the wall. You might have to cut off 2 inches or more from the width of a panel of plywood, but it is easier to do it near the wall than in the center of the room where the discrepancy is more noticeable.

CHIMNEYS AND CEILINGS

If you plan to install a fireplace in your house, you need to make plans for framing the rough opening for the chimney to extend through the ceiling and roof. The most obvious question is that of the location of the fireplace and chimney.

Many people prefer to construct the chimney on the outside wall of the house. There are several good reasons for doing so. One reason is safety. If there should be a chimney fire, the chances are good that less damage will occur if the chimney is on the outside of the house.

Many fire experts have stated that it is actually the second fire rather than the first one that does the damage. The theory is that the first chimney fire creates such intense heat inside the chimney that the chimney liners are cracked or the mortar between liner sections is heated until it disintegrates. Even though the fire is either extinguished or allowed to burn itself out, the crack remains, and the next time there is a chimney fire the intense heat attacks the wood framing of the floor or ceiling or roof rafters and a chimney fire becomes a house fire. If the crack in the liner is on the side of the chimney that is in contact with wood, the chances of a fire are much greater. There is also the probability that the crack will be on one of the three sides of the chimney not in direct contact with wood.

If the chimney is located in the center of the house, there will be wood in direct contact on all four sides of the chimney and the chance of fire obviously becomes greater. Some fire fighters have also stated that there is a greater chance of extensive damage if the fire occurs in the center of the house rather than on one end. Still others point out that if there is a need to make repairs to the chimney, the work is done more easily and less expensively if the chimney is on the outside of the house.

There are also arguments for locating the chimney on the inside of the house. One is that the same chimney can be used for back-to-back fireplaces in adjoining rooms and even additional fireplaces upstairs. You can save hundreds, perhaps thousands, of dollars by locating more than one fireplace on the same chimney rather than building more than one chimney.

Whatever your choice of location, if you include a chimney in your house, you must frame around the rough opening. If the chimney is to be located on the outside wall, the framing must be done in the floor as well as in the ceiling and roof. If you are constructing a two-story house, you will have to frame in the floor of the first story, the floor of the second story, the ceiling of the second story, and the roof.

Many building experts contend that the greatest economy in building can be found in the two-story house. The reason is that you can double your floor space simply by adding the cost of materials and labor for extra wall framing and flooring. The foundations will cost as much for one story as for two, as will the roof and other basics. It has been estimated that the second story costs only one-third per square foot than a one-story costs. These estimates are subject to variables such as whether you do the labor or hire someone, the types or grades of materials used, and so on.

When you are framing for a chimney on the outside of the house, you will have to cut or eliminate the header section that would normally have proceeded along the wall lines. You will also have to pour additional footings or pads for the chimney. Be sure to pour the footings or pads generously with concrete, because an immense amount of weight will be upon this small expanse of sand, gravel, and cement.

Your foundation wall will have to accommodate the chimney framing. The indentation should be deep enough to allow for the interior fireplace and hearth.

Instead of a straight-line header, make two right angles along the wall line and two at the back of the chimney allowance. At the point where the wall-line header is cut, nail the header timbers to the end of the existing header timber. Use four 20-penny nails in the 2-×-6 or 2-×-8 timbers, but do not drive them near enough to the edge to split the wood.

Do the same at the other side of the chimney location. The two timbers used should be exactly the same length.

At the back of the chimney allowance space, nail the final header timber section so that the ends of the final section abut the ends of the first two timbers installed. Again, use four 20-penny nails.

You will need no other support for the header framing than the foundation wall and the footings already poured. Use only the soundest of materials in these locations. Use ample bridging to help strengthen the framing. Abut joists to the modified header line as you would have if it had been a straight wall line (FIG. 4-11).

4-11 When framing around a fireplace or chimney, this type of structure gives good support.

At the ceiling line, if the chimney is to become a part of the wall line, you will need to frame another indentation. You can actually allow the chimney to run up the side of the house without altering the framing of the ceiling lines. If the chimney is part of the wall—that is, if it runs up the outside of the house—you will have to do weatherproofing in the areas where the wall and chimney meet. If the wall is already constructed and the chimney runs up the wall itself, there will be no problem with sealing the lines.

The advantage of having the chimney become part of the wall is that you will have the attractive look of brickwork as part of the walls of the room affected by the chimney. You can also install gypsum board or Sheetrock over the bricks if you decide later that you do not want them as part of the wall.

Chapter 5

Roof framing

*T*he obvious purposes of a roof are simple: to keep out the rain and other precipitation and to protect against the cold. The part of the country in which you live will greatly determine the type of roof you intend to frame. For example, where there is a great deal of snow accumulation, there is usually a need for greater slope to the roof. This slope is often called the roof pitch.

There are several types of basic roof styles: the gable, the lean-to or shed roof, the hip roof, and the valley roof. Often there are combinations of these basic types.

ROOF TYPES

The gable roof is formed by two sloping walls which meet at the center of the building—the highest point. The gable roof is easy to construct, simple in concept, and economical. The gable roof can be used on virtually any type of structure and offers no real complications. It is easy to seal against leaking. The gable roof can be installed by two or more workers or by a single person, with the help of the suggestions in this chapter (FIG. 5-1).

The lean-to or shed roof has its high point at the front of the building and slopes straight toward the back of the building. Often the shed roof is held up by posts and nails on the front side and by the back wall. This is perhaps the easiest of all roof types to frame. It is also economical.

The hip roof—unlike the gable roof which has two slopes and the shed roof which has only one slope—has four slopes, one for each of the four walls. The high point of the roof is in the center of the building and the supporting rafters must be installed diagonally so that they meet in the center of the roof.

The valley roof, also called the gable and valley roof, has two gables that intersect with each other. The valley is the intersection of the two roof lines at the bottom of the slope. This type of roof is more difficult to frame and slightly more expensive in terms of the extra materials needed.

5-1   A gable roof is one of the simplest of all types of roof construction.

Few roof lines are perfectly flat, although there are some that have no slope at all. The slope is necessary for shedding water. A flat roof will permit standing water or snow, which can eventually find its way into the attic or living area of the building.

A DESCRIPTION OF TERMS

The *span* of the roof is that distance from top plate to top plate or rafter seats. The total *rise* of the roof refers to the distance from the peak of the roof to the top plates. The *run* of the roof refers to the level distance over which any rafter will pass. This distance is normally half the span distance, because the rafter leading to the peak of the roof will cover only half of the level distance below.

A *rafter* is any of the main pieces of timber that make up the main part of the roof. Rafters normally are attached at their lowest point to the top plate of a wall frame and to the ridgepole in older buildings. In more modern terminology, the ridgepole refers to the ridgeboard, simply because poles are rarely, if ever, used in roofing practices today.

The *ridgeboard* is the long timber that runs the length of the roof at the highest level of the roof frame. This long timber serves to form the peak, along with the rafters that are joined to it as they run from the top cap upward at a slant or pitch (FIG. 5-2).

Common rafters are those timbers that, as mentioned above, connect the ridgeboard to the top cap. These rafters are, in almost all cases, connected at right angles to the ridgeboard.

Where a combination of roof types has been used, there are certain rafters that run from the top plate or top cap to the ridgeboard at the places where the two roof lines intersect. These are called valley rafters because they are installed in the valley, or the point where the roof lines meet at their lowest level.

Hip rafters extend diagonally from the top plate or top cap to the ridgeboard. They run from the outside corners which are formed by perpendicular plates to the ridgeboard.

Where the rafters join the top cap or top plate, several cuts are made to permit the ends of the rafters to join smoothly. These cuts are called seat, bottom, or heel cuts. At the top or ridgeboard end of the rafters, the cuts that are made so the rafters will fit evenly against the ridgeboard are called top or plumb cuts.

Before you consider laying out your rafters, you may, if you choose to do so, install the top caps over the top plates of the wall frame. These top caps are only 2 × 4s that are nailed to the top plates and are installed perfectly flush with the edges of the plates. These caps lap over all spliced sections and add double strength to that portion of the wall frame. One of the major functions of the top cap is to negate the weaknesses created in the top plate where two 2 × 4s are butt-jointed.

If you decide to extend the rafters over the plate or cap lines (usually at a distance of 1 foot), that part of the rafter forming the overhang is the eave or tail of the rafter. The term "rafter length" refers to the shortest distance between the outer edge of the top plate or top cap and the center of the ridge line.

The purpose of eaves in a roof is to channel water down the slope or pitch of the roof and fall to the ground a foot or so from the wall of the building. Because of the eaves, runoff water does not come in contact with the walls unless there is a high wind blowing directly toward the

5-2 A good ridgeboard is one of the most important elements of good roof construction.

building. While this might seem a trivial part of roofing, remember that water running off the roof carries with it staining materials from the roofing that can discolor the walls of the building. This staining is particularly noticeable if the walls are red brick or if they are painted white.

CALCULATING PITCH

The amount of pitch or slope of a roof is often referred to in terms of fractional amounts that are equivalent to inches of actual rise in the roof line. A 1/6 pitch is equal to a 4-inch rise per unit of run or roof distance. A 1/4 pitch equals 6 inches of rise, while a $1/3$ pitch means that the roof will rise 8 inches per unit of run or roof distance. A $5/12$ pitch means a 10-inch rise; $1/2$ pitch a 12-inch rise; $5/8$ pitch a 15-inch rise; $3/4$ pitch an 18-inch rise. A pitch of 1 means a rise of 2 feet per unit of rise.

When you are preparing to cut rafters for the roof, consult your house plans. If you are working without plans or with incomplete or poorly detailed plans, you will need to calculate how long your rafters will need to be. To do so, use a tape measure and measure from the outside edge of the top plate or cap to the outside edge of the top plate or cap on the opposite side of the house frame. Use a tape measure because a folding ruler or similar device is subject to too many possibilities of errors.

Once you have determined the first distance, divide that distance in half, because the rafters will not reach all the way across the expanse unless you are constructing a shed or lean-to roof. Half of the distance is then the horizontal distance the rafters will cover. If the building is 24 feet wide from outside edges of the top plates, your horizontal distance will be 12 feet.

You must now take into consideration the amount of pitch or rise the roof will have. This rise will greatly affect the length of the rafters. A carpenter's square (SEE SIDEBAR) will help you determine rise and rafter length fairly easily.

Assume you want a rise of 4 inches per foot for your roof. On the tongue of the carpenters square find the 4. (The tongue is the short part of the square.) This figure represents the number of inches of rise per foot you want. Now measure from the 4 on the outside edge of the tongue to the 12 on the outside edge of the blade of the square. The blade is the long part of the square. Assume that the distance is $12^3/4$ inches.

The run of the rafter is 12 feet (half the distance between the outside edges of the top plates), so you will need to multiply the $12^3/4$ figure by 12. That figure will be 153, the number of inches in the rafter. Divide by 12 to determine the number of feet in a rafter and you will find that each common rafter must be measured at 12 feet, 9 inches long.

The extra length (as opposed to the 12 feet of horizontal distance) allows for the rise of 4 inches per foot over the 12-foot distance. To be safe, you can make a tentative measurement and cut one rafter to be certain that you did not make a mistake anywhere in your calculations. Once you are certain that you are correct, you can determine the plumb and seat cuts.

If you plan to have an overhang or eaves, you need to add 12 inches to the length of the rafters. The figure you calculated does not include any eave allowance at all.

CUTTING THE RAFTERS

Now make the plumb cut of the rafter. Add the 12 inches for the eave, if you have not done so, and then mark where the rafter will normally end. Using the sample rafter measurement, you will need 12 feet, 9 inches. The

Carpenter's Square

If you are a beginning carpenter or home repairman, you might not own a carpenter's square. If not, you will find one to have many uses, and they are not expensive to buy. It will pay you to have one before you progress very far with your do-it-yourself work.

The most common use of the square is for testing the trueness of an angle or for making a perfectly straight right-angle mark across a board or other lumber for a later cut. You align the blade of the square with the edge of the timber to be marked. In this fashion you can determine whether the lumber has a straight edge. Once you are assured that it does, you will see that the tongue of the square extends across the board at a perfect right angle.

The typical carpenter's square has a tongue that is 12 inches long and a blade that is 24 inches long. The size of this instrument will permit you to mark the widest boards and to allow you to mark, by moving the square once or twice, even the 4-×-8 foot plywood panels or Sheetrock.

To mark the wider panels of building materials, align the tongue of the square with the edge of the panel and allow the blade to extend its full length across the panel. Mark along the top or outside edge of the blade. Then move the square so that the blade lies along the final 6 inches of the mark and extends 18 inches beyond the mark.

Because the top of the blade is aligned with the final part of the first mark, you know that you are extending the mark line in a straight fashion. Mark the rest of the blade length and then repeat the process, if necessary, across the remainder of the panel. Using this process, you can mark the entire length of the longest timbers you will encounter, if you should need to trim one over a long expanse or stretch.

Angle-marking is not the only purpose of the square. The figures on the square tongue and blade will enable you to make rather complicated woodworking computations with great speed and ease. You can figure numerous angles and mark the cuts by using the square.

You can also test for flatness of a surface by standing the square on edge. Lay the edge of the blade on the surface to be tested and hold the square erect by the tongue. If any light shows under the blade edge, the surface is not totally flat.

If you are trimming a surface, hold the square in the manner described above and you can see where the irregularities are. As you trim, continue to use the square to check. If a door or other moving item will not close or seat properly, the square will show you where the problem area is and when it has been properly corrected.

cut you are about to make will be the angle cut where the rafter will be nailed to the ridgeboard (FIG. 5-3).

Select a sound, straight rafter that is as true as you can find. Do not use a bowed or crooked rafter for this very crucial cut. Lay the rafter on its

5-3 When nailing rafters to a ridgeboard, stagger the rafter ends slightly for a better nailing surface.

side. For best results, the rafter should be on sawhorses or work benches so that the work can be done while you are standing in a comfortable position.

Hold the square so that the tongue is in your left hand and the blade is in your right hand. The heel (or "corner" of the square) should be pointed away from your body. Lay the square as close to the end of the rafter as you can get it. The heel, or corner, should be at the end of the rafter unless there is a defect that would render that part of the rafter useless.

You earlier chose a 4-inch rise per foot, so you will need to place the square so that the 4-inch mark on the tongue and the 12$^3/4$ mark on the blade are on the edge of what will become the top of the rafter. The 12$^3/4$ figure is the length of the rafter that you calculated earlier (12 feet, 9 inches). The heel of the square should be even with the opposite edge of the rafter.

Hold the square in place and mark along the outside edge of the tongue. This is where your plumb cut will be made. When the rafter is held against the ridgeboard, the surface you just marked (and will later cut) will fit flush against the ridgeboard. You will have a good nailing surface as well as the accurate pitch or slope for your roof (FIG. 5-4).

Many people do not bother making plumb cuts for the eave end of the rafter. You might elect to make the cuts, because it will be much easier to nail a boxing board or similar timber in place later. If so, go to the other end of the rafter, the end opposite the one you just marked and will later cut, and mark again.

Measure the correct length of your rafter, remembering to add the eaves section of one extra foot, and mark the point where the rafter is 12$^3/4$ feet long. Hold the square so that the 4-inch mark on the tongue is directly on the 12$^3/4$ mark and mark as you did earlier. The cut you make will be plumb.

Now you need to calculate and mark the bird's-mouth cut or the level cut for the plate or top cap. This is for the seat of the rafter so that it can rest on the top plate neatly and in a secure and well-fitted manner. Use the bird's-mouth cut only if you plan to have a projection of the rafter over the eaves. If the rafter ends at the top plate, only use a plumb cut or seat cut.

Think of the bird's-mouth cut only as a notch in the bottom of the rafter that will allow the rafter to be seated securely onto the top plate or cap. The depth of the bird's-mouth cut is dependent upon the level you wish for the heel cut. If you cut the bird's-mouth notch deeply enough, there will be very little room between the rafter bottom and the top of the plate. The more shallow the cut, the more room there will be.

Lay off the bird's-mouth notch cut in the same manner used for the plumb cuts. Measure off the depth you want, and then use the square heel or corner to mark for the cut. You want the horizontal cut to be parallel with the top of the plate and the vertical cut to be parallel with the edge of the plate (FIG. 5-5).

5-4   A good flush fit of rafter against ridgeboard is important in roof framing.

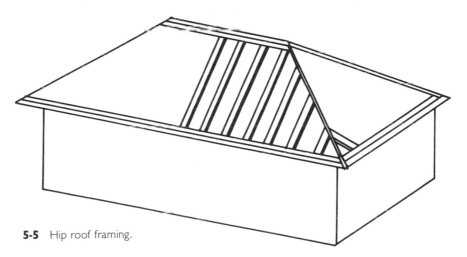

5-5   Hip roof framing.

You might want to try the bird's-mouth cut on a scrap piece of lumber before you risk trying it on a rafter. A rafter that is very long is a costly unit of lumber and you do not want to risk ruining one. If you do damage the end of a rafter, you can still use the remainder of the timber for studding, top capping, or other work requiring 2-×-4 lumber.

HIP RAFTER LAYOUT

Remember that hip rafters extend diagonally from the outside corners to the ridgeboard. Most hip roof types are called equal-pitch roofs. This means that the angles or slopes or pitches of all four sides of the roof are equal. The pitch of the front and back are the same as the slope of the sides (FIG. 5-5).

Determine the length of hip roof rafters in much the same way as you did common rafters. You must use the so-called "bridge measure" times the unit or length of the run.

To figure out the length of the hip rafters, first make a scale drawing of the roof and determine the width of the entire building. Once you have drawn a rough diagram of the exterior measurements of the roof, draw a line precisely down the center of the rectangle. This line must be equidistant from both long sides. Next, draw two lines across the rectangle. The first line should be from a point one-third of the way down the rectangle to a point on the opposite side that is also one-third of the way down the building outline. The next line should be placed at the two-thirds point. Mark from the outside corners of the rectangle to the angles formed by the lines at one-third and two-thirds the length of the rectangle. This is assuming that all four roof pitches will be the same. They will not be the same unless all six segments of the rectangle are the same (FIG. 5-6).

If you label the lines, you can follow the diagram better. Let the upper left corner of the rectangle be labeled A; the upper right B; the lower left C, and the lower right D. The center line ends will become E and F, for the left juncture and the right one, respectively. The lines crossing the rectangle and the center lines are G and H for the left line and I and J for the right line, with G and I on the upper edge of the rectangle. The point where the line crosses the lengthwise line at the left of the rectangle is K and where the other line crosses is L. You can label any way you wish; this is simply a sample method that allows simplification later, when juncture references are made.

The lone line down the center is the ridgeboard. You will notice that ridge-end rafters labeled AK, EK, BK, IK, and HK will all join the ridgeboard at the same point. On the other end of the rectangle, rafters GL, CL, DL, FL, and JL will all join the ridgeboard at the same location.

In the center sections of the rectangle, the two squares will need common rafters, each of which will cover one-half of the total span of the building. The four rafters that form the triangles will all be the same length.

Figuring the length of the hip rafters in a hip roof is rather complicated in its most complex mathematical form. You know that the com-

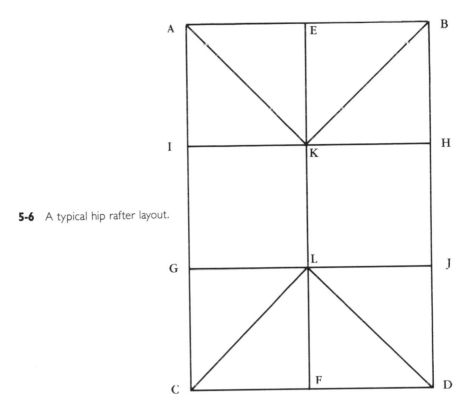

5-6 A typical hip rafter layout.

mon rafter must cover one half the total span, and if you are working on a building that is 30 feet wide, one-half the span is 15 feet. The total run of the hip rafter, then, is the square root of the sum of the square footage lengths of the two common rafters.

In a simpler sense, square the length of the first rafter. The rafter is 15 feet long, and the square of 15 is 225 feet. Add the square of the other rafter, also 225 feet, and the total is 450 feet. Take the square root of 450, and the answer is roughly 21.21.

You can insert the calculations for deciding the rise of the building by using the formula given earlier in this chapter. If you decide that the total rise of the roof slope is 5 feet, you can then figure out the lengths of the hip rafters by squaring 21.21 and then adding the square of 5—the total rise—and then taking the square root of the sums.

The square of 21.21 is 449.8641, and if you add the square of the rise, you will have a total of 474.8641. Now use a pocket calculator and take the square root of the last figure, and the answer is 21.79 or 21.8 feet.

There are simpler ways to figure lengths of both hip rafters and common rafters, and these will be discussed in the next section. Many, if not most, do-it-yourselfers have found that the simpler the methods are, the greater the enjoyment of the work and the better the finished product.

Once the lengths of the hip rafters have been determined, you can calculate the lengths of the remainder of the rafters in the section of the roof. These will become progressively shorter as you move from the center of the house span to the outer edges.

If you allow an eaves projection on hip rafters, you do not simply add 12 inches to the total length of the rafter. The hip rafter extends at an angle and must be longer than 12 inches in order for it to extend far enough to be even with the rafter ends of the side and end of the building.

Figure the overhang by squaring the length of the overhang of the common rafter, doubling that sum, and finding the square root of the final figure. You are actually finding the hypotenuse of the triangle formed by the extension of the common rafter and the extension of the hip rafter. If the common rafter extends or has an eave length of 12 inches, square that figure and the result is 144 inches. Now double the 144 and you have 288 inches. Take the square root of that figure and you will get 16.97 inches.

When you are ready to cut the ends of the hip rafters, note that common rafters meet the ridgeboard at right angles. The cut is slanted but squarely marked across the end of the rafter. The hip rafter does not meet the ridgeboard at a 90-degree angle, but is instead 45 degrees. The problem is compounded when you realize that the hip rafter will meet another hip rafter at the ridgepole at the same point.

You will need to stand the rafter on edge and place the tongue of the square along the line of the ridge cut. Measure and mark off one-half of the rafter edge. Now set the tongue of the square so that you can mark off the opposite half of the rafter edge. You have already made your plumb cuts, and now you can cut the rafter end so that you have a slightly slanted cut with two beveled sides. You will have a fitting that will work very well for you at this point.

CALCULATING RAFTER LENGTHS

As indicated earlier, if you dislike the mathematical methods of calculating rafter length, there are alternatives. When you first marked a cut for a common rafter, you were told how to use the carpenter's square to mark a perfect plumb cut. You held the tongue of the square in your right hand and the blade in your left hand, with the heel of the square pointing away from your body. The rafter is lying on its side before you.

Using the methods described earlier, set the square in the proper position so that the tongue is exactly on the lower corner of the rafter end and the blade is at the prescribed position, depending upon the slope or rise of your roof line. Mark where the blade crosses the edge of the rafter. The mark should be on the outside edge of the blade. Now move the square and reposition it exactly as you did before, with the mark representing the lower corner of the rafter. Mark where the blade leaves the edge of the rafter again. Each time you move the square, you have performed one step.

Continue to step off the units until you have completed marking the rafter. There will be the same number of steps in the rafter length as there are feet in the run. Remember that the run is the total distance in the span that will be covered by the rafter. If the building is 30 feet from plate to plate, the span is 30 feet. Half of that is 15. The run, then, is 15 feet. If your building has a run of 15 feet, mark off 15 steps with the square and you have the length of your rafter.

This method is not mathematically exact, but it is workable. As with all cuts, however, you are urged to mark the rafter and hold it in place to see that it will work well for the span you are covering. If it works, use that rafter as a pattern for all cuts.

Some carpenters use the "stepping off" method even for hip rafters. They use, instead of a 12-inch setting, a 17-inch run setting. This means that you will set the square differently from the way you did with the 12-inch setting for a common rafter and use the 17-inch setting instead, with a different step for each foot of span or run covered by the rafter.

Yet another alternative is the old-fashioned but highly accurate method of spot-marking. In this method nothing is left to chance. When you are cutting common rafters, you lay the rafter over the top plate or top cap, then climb up and hold one end of the rafter so that the bottom edge rests on the top of the ridgeboard. Be sure that the point of the rafter resting on the ridgeboard is as near the end of the rafter as you can manage without having the rafter fall off.

With the rafter in place, hold the carpenter's square so that the back of the blade is firmly positioned against the side or cheek of the ridgeboard. The blade will extend past the width of the rafter. Mark the rafter along the outside edge of the square blade. Your plumb cut line will be exact (FIG. 5-7). While this method requires more time, in a sense, than

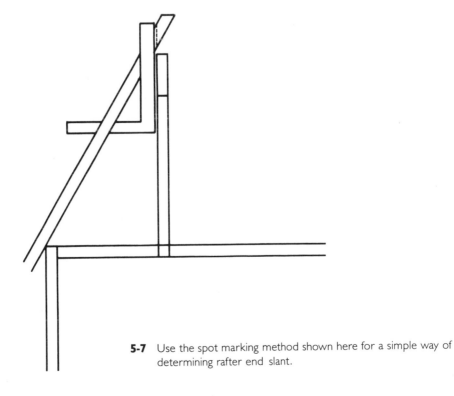

5-7 Use the spot marking method shown here for a simple way of determining rafter end slant.

does the computation method, it allows for fewer mistakes. Your major problems will be climbing up to the ridgeboard and holding the rafter in place while you mark it.

Next, cut the rafter and sink one nail through the cut and at an angle, just as if you were nailing it into the ridgeboard. Then climb back to the ridgeboard and nail the rafter in place, but only temporarily. Once you are certain that it is in its proper position, climb down and use a level to mark the eaves end of the rafter.

If you want a bird's-mouth cut follow this procedure: While the rafter is resting on the top of the top plate or cap, hold your level so that one side of it is flush against the edge of the top plate and the bubble in the level shows a true vertical position. Mark along the edge of the level so the line is a continuation of the line of the outside edge of the plate.

Assuming that you want the end to be cut so that it is vertically true, hold the level until the bubble shows a true vertical position. Then mark along the edge of the level, just as if it were a square. Now you can take down the rafter, make the cuts, and use that rafter as a pattern for all future cuts.

You can now complete the bird's-mouth cut. Earlier you marked a line corresponding with the line formed by the outside edge of the plate. Now decide how deep you want the cut to be. If you want it to be 1 inch deep, measure up the bird's-mouth cut line 1 inch and mark the location. Then use your square so that the blade of the square forms a right angle to the line that corresponds to the line of the outside edge of the plate. Mark along the blade of the square to the edge of the rafter (FIG. 5-8).

If your plate is installed properly, you will have a perfect fit at the bird's-mouth location and at the ridgeboard. Position the rafter, and if it fits to your satisfaction, cut others by this pattern and install them.

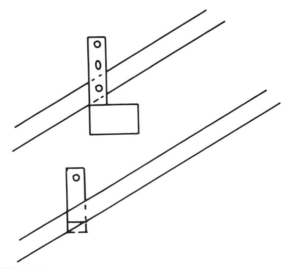

5-8 Methods of determining an accurate bird's-mouth cut.

Theoretically, any rafters that will fit on one side of the house will fit on the other, if the ridgeboard is installed in the exact center of the house so that the span on each side is exactly the same length. It is risky to assume that the distance is the same. It is best to try a pattern-cut rafter first and check if it fits the opposite side. If it does, then you can cut and install the others.

When you are cutting hip rafters, you can use much the same process, with some variations, as used above. You can place the hip rafter to be marked so that one end rests upon the plate just above the corner post. The other end should extend slightly past the end of the ridgeboard.

Stand the rafter on edge and let the lower edge rest on the top of the ridgeboard so that the outside edge of the rafter is even with the outside edge of the ridgeboard. The rafter will meet the ridgeboard at an angle. You can then reach under the rafter and use a pencil mark along the underside of the rafter, holding the pencil against the ridgeboard. The mark will give you one of the angle cuts for the rafter. Mark along the top of the rafter to correspond with the end of the ridgeboard.

Now mark from either an imaginary or real mark along the center of the top of the ridgeboard. Let the line continue across the top of the rafter until it runs off the edge. These marks, if you saw along them, will give you all of the fitting cuts needed to install the rafter at the ridgepole.

If you want an overhang for the hip rafters but do not feel comfortable with the Pythagorean theorem, there is a simple way to achieve a perfect ending for your hip rafter overhangs. With the hip rafter nailed temporarily in place so that you can mark for the cuttings, toe nail—also temporarily—a 12-inch section of 2 × 4 to the outer edge of the plate. It can be as close as you like to the corner. Then hold a length of board or 2 × 4 so that one end is flush with the end of the 12-inch piece and the other end passes under or above the hip rafter, but is in actual contact with the hip rafter.

Mark along the inside of the board and across the end of the hip rafter. You have thus squared the corner and marked the length of the hip rafter. You have actually squared only one side of the hip rafter. If you want to square the other side, repeat the process. You will note that the two lines cross each other halfway across the hip rafter. Cut accordingly and you will bevel the end of the hip rafter. Mark for the plumb cut and that corner of the building is completed, as far as the measurement and cutting of rafters is concerned.

This sounds like a great deal of trouble, but actually it all can be taken care of within a short time. When you have marked and cut one hip rafter, use it as a pattern for both sides of the house. If it works, cut another rafter, and half of this particular job is completed.

When you are ready to install other rafters along the hip line, use the same process. Lay the ends of rafters over the hip rafter and mark along the hip rafter lines. You can get your slant cut and plumb cut from one marking. Remember, when you mark and cut one rafter for the hip roof, you can cut another the same and it will correspond with the other side of the hip slope on that wall of the house.

If your roof lines are the same dimensions on both ends of the opposite sides of a hip roof, instead of cutting two rafters from one marking, you can cut four. Two will be used on the same roof line and the other two will be used on the opposite roof line. Space the rafters as you did the joists and studs. If you make it a practice of spacing everything in the walls, floors, and roof so that you have 16-inch centers, you will eliminate problems with installing sheathing and other wall, floor, and roof coverings.

INSTALLING VALLEY RAFTERS

Wherever two roof lines meet, whether at two different roof slopes or where a dormer has been installed, you will want to install valley rafters. The *valley* is the lowest point where the two roof lines meet.

The valley rafter is measured, marked, cut, and installed in much the same fashion as the hip rafter. The valley rafter will have a double-side cut at the tail, while the hip rafter has only a single cut. The hip rafter tail or plate end is square cut or plumb cut, but the valley rafter must fit into two angles because it forms the hypotenuse of the triangle. Whatever is done to one of the two triangles formed by a roof line or dormer will be done to the other side, so your marking and cutting is done in a double fashion. That is, one rafter will serve as the pattern for its counterpart on the other side of the dormer or roof line.

In the case of dormers, the dormer lines are shorter than full-length roof lines would be, and slight modifications must be made for the installation of dormers. You will probably want to install a valley rafter that will be the same length as a full roof line rafter on one side of the dormer, and then install the second dormer rafter so that it connects with the full-length rafter just installed.

As mentioned earlier, the equal span roof is far more common than the unequal span types, and with obvious reasons. It is far more difficult to frame the roof if the slopes and spans are different for the various sections of the roof, and you will be wise to keep the span distance equal on all types of valley roof layouts, whether you plan to install dormers or gables.

Start with a typical roof framing layout by assuming that the main body of the building to be roofed is 20 feet wide, with the gable to be erected on one of the long sides of the building. The first step is to run the ridgeboard down the length of the building so that you will have 10-foot spans on each side of the ridgeboard.

Your building has been divided in half by the ridgeboard. Now divide the half on which the gable will be installed into thirds. You will have a common rafter that will run the length of the span from the outer edge of the plate to the ridgeboard. Label the point where the common rafter leaves the plate as A. Label the point where the rafter connects with the ridgeboard as B. The label C is assigned to the midpoint in the length of the ridgeboard, and D is assigned to the midpoint in the length of the plate.

Rafter A left the plate at a position that is one-third of the length of the plate. Rafter D left the plate at the halfway point. Rafter E will leave the plate at the three-fourths point and will, like rafter A, intersect with the ridgeboard at right angles. Rafters F and G will run diagonally from the plate to the ridgeboard and divide the squares on each side of the midpoint into two triangles of the same size.

You will then need to run a ridgeboard along the length of the gable or dormer from the primary ridgeboard to the edge of the plate. If you are building dormers rather than gables, then the secondary ridgeboard need not run all the way to the plate edge. The span of the gable is often the same as the span of the basic part of the building.

Make side cuts for the gable rafters because they intersect with the main ridgeboard. Also make double side cuts for the valley rafter tail because it intersects with two other timbers and must fit into the V or right angle of the juncture points.

Common rafters are later added between the valley rafters and the ridgeboard, but these will have to be slant cut on both ends—one cut for the plumb juncture with the ridgeboard and the other for the juncture with the common rafter.

If your gable span is shorter than the span of the basic roof line, you can frame the gable in the following manner. Because the pitch of the two roof lines will be the same, the ridgeboard and the roof line of the gable or dormer will be lower than the roof line of the main building.

As suggested earlier, run the common rafters from the plate to the ridgeboard until you reach the point where the gable or dormer valley rafters are to be installed. Then run a valley rafter from the plate to the primary ridgeboard. Think of the plate end of the rafter as A and the ridgeboard end of the rafter as B. Then think of a second valley rafter with the plate end as C and the other end as D. Mark, cut, and nail the second valley rafter to the plate. The other end is similarly attached to the first valley rafter you installed to form a wide V, with the open end of the V at the plate. You are now ready to proceed with the basic framing of the gable.

You can also frame the gable or dormer by running a common rafter down the center of the dormer line, starting at the plate and ending at the ridgeboard. Then valley rafters of equal length are run from the plate to the common rafter you just installed. You will have to slant cut both ends of the valley rafters in order to attach them smoothly to the common rafter.

INSTALLING JACK RAFTERS

By definition, a *jack rafter* is any rafter that is a part of a common rafter but is shortened in order to frame it to a valley rafter, a hip rafter, or both valley and hip rafters. Often the rafters that are framed to a hip rafter are called *hip jacks*, and those framed to valley rafters are called *valley jacks*. The short rafters that are attached to either valley rafters or hip rafters are called *cripple jacks*, either valley cripple jacks or hip valley cripple jacks.

The term "cripple" is very similar in its concept to the short studs under windows in wall framing. These short studs are called *cripple studs*.

When you are framing the gable or dormer, you should double the common rafters that are the last ones before the gable or dormer framing begins. You will have double common rafters on each side of the gable or dormer.

You will have a header that is preferably doubled (as are the common rafters), at the beginning of the dormer, or on the opening of the dormer near the plate. The secondary ridgeboard will extend from the pitch of the roof in a horizontal line toward the plate. The valley rafters will be attached to the upper header, which is also doubled, where the dormer blends into the basic roof line. You will then have double headers at the upper and lower extremes of the dormer.

There will be an empty triangle between the double common rafters and the pitch of the dormer. This triangle will be reinforced by the installation of jack rafters.

Space the jack rafters as you spaced all common rafters, on a basic 16-inch center. One end of the jack rafter will be nailed to the upper header. The end cut is simply a square cut, because there is no slant to deal with. The end of the rafter that will be nailed to the lower header must be slant cut or beveled.

Mark these cut lines by holding the uncut length of rafter timber so that one end is even with the inside edge of the upper header and the other end lies over the top of the valley rafter that runs from the juncture of the lower header and the double common rafters. By looking down upon the point where the valley jack crosses over the valley rafter, you can mark the top of the valley jack.

When you have made the preliminary marking, use your square to mark the side or cheek of the rafter. If you are using a circular saw, adjust the angle of the blade until it corresponds with the angle of the mark, then saw the end of the valley jack. You might want to experiment with a scrap piece of lumber the same thickness as that of the valley jack before you try it on the timber you are going to install.

If your circular saw will not adjust to the angle you need, start the cut with the circular saw and finish it with a hand saw. Mark and cut all other jack rafters in the triangle and install them. These short jack rafters are called *main roof valley jacks*.

You now have the secondary ridgeboard as it extends from the juncture with the upper header and ends above the lower header. You will need to mark, cut, and install dormer valley jacks in both slopes of the dormer.

Between the upper header and the primary ridgeboard you will have an empty rectangle that is to be filled in with short common rafters. These are called *cripple common rafters*. No slant cuts are needed for any of the cripples. Simply measure from the upper edge of the double upper header to the inside edge of the ridgeboard, and mark, cut, and install.

Below the lower header you will need to fill in the narrow rectangle between the double common rafters and the lower header. These short timbers are also called cripple common rafters. They will be straight cut for the upper attachment to the lower header and plumb cut on the end that extends over the plate. You will also need a bird's-mouth notch on the cripples where they fit over the plate.

Use the same pattern you used when you laid out the common rafters for the bird's-mouth cut. Make the cut on a scrap piece of lumber and try it to be sure you are still accurate with measurements. If the sample cut fits to your total satisfaction, cut all of the cripple common rafters and install them. Be sure to space them 16 inches on-center, as with all the other rafters.

Chapter **6**

Sheathing and bracing

Before you begin to sheathe your roof, be sure that all bracing and other support work has been properly done. The roof will need to keep out cold, heat, and moisture during every hour of every day of the year, and a poorly constructed roof can be easily damaged.

One of the greatest dangers to a roof is wind. In stormy weather, high winds can rip a roof completely off a building that is only months old, while a short distance away an old barn that has stood empty for decades resists the storm easily. The difference is in the material of the roof and how the roof was installed. If good roofing material is attached well to sound roof framing, the roof is able to withstand great pressure, but a poorly installed roof is more of a liability than an asset.

Snow is another major cause of roof damage. Snow, when it has accumulated to a depth of several inches, creates considerable pressure across the entire expanse of a roof. There is not one inch of space that does not receive the pressure. When the pressure of the weight of the snow remains on the roof for several days, any weak roof points will start to sag or bow, and soon the melting snow will find its way into the attic and from there into the living quarters of the house. As it enters the house, the water can cause considerable damage to the ceiling. Often the ceiling tile or gypsum board begins to disintegrate because of the dampness. The greatest and costliest damage over a period of time is not to the ceiling, however, but to the studding and rafters and to interior walls. When the moisture trickles down the rafters, then to the studding, and finally to the sole plate and sills and joists, the damage is severe.

Moisture also encourages insects to live and breed in the timbers of a house. Generally, there is a need for at least a 20 percent moisture content in the wood for insects and decay to do damage.

Therefore, before you install sheathing, you will need to check for any signs of instability that could lead to roof weakness and eventually to costly damage. One of the first places to check is the points where rafters, valley rafters, valley jacks, and other timbers are attached to the ridgeboards and other higher points.

A major cause of weakness at these juncture points is faulty nailing, which in turn is often caused by improper marking and cutting of connecting timbers. In this chapter, suggestions will be provided for the sturdy nailing of all roof elements and for the installation of braces that will keep the roof from giving or weakening in high winds or under heavy pressure from weight on the roof.

INSTALLING RIDGEBOARDS

One of the common methods of installing a ridgeboard is for two people to hold it in position while others lift the end common rafters in position and nail them to the ridgeboard. If you are working alone, you will experience considerable difficulty in attempting to install the ridgeboard. You can do the job, but you will need some help from a simple device called a ridgeboard raiser.

First, you need to know the exact height of the roof above the top plate or top cap. To figure the height, find out the amount of rise per foot of your roof slope or pitch. Consult Chapter 5 for details on how to calculate rafter lengths and related material for roof pitch.

If your roof is to rise 4 inches per foot, and if the distance of half the span of the entire main body of the house is 12 feet, you know that your roof slope or pitch is 12 times 4, or 48 inches. If the rise is 6 inches per foot, your ridge height will be 72 inches. Figure the rise not on the running foot length of the common rafters but on the horizontal distance from the outer edge of the top plate to the exact center of the house, and then deduct half the thickness of the ridgeboard. When you have arrived at the exact height of the ridgeboard, locate two 2-×-4 or 1-×-5 boards (actually, any straight timbers will work) and lay them so that the ends are even. Then measure down the width of the ridgeboard and nail a short length of 2 × 4 at exact right angles with the two timbers you have laid out.

Assume that the ridgeboard is $5^1/2$ inches wide. At a point $5^1/2$ inches below the ends of the two timbers, nail the short piece of scrap material, but separate the two long timbers by the thickness of the ridgeboard. If the ridgeboard is 2 inches thick, lay the timbers 2 inches apart, and allow a slight margin—perhaps $1/4$ inch or so. At the other ends of the timbers, nail a similar piece across them. You need not measure or try to be exact. This length is only to make the timbers more manageable. If you have the timbers to spare, make two of these raisers, one for each end of the ridgeboard (FIG. 6-1). You can use these timbers again, after the ridgeboard is in place.

Measure and mark down from the end of the raiser the distance equal to the height of the roof above the ridgeboard. Nail the raiser in place so that the mark for the roof height is level with the top of the plate and the end with the $2^1/2$ opening extends vertically upward. Nail the raiser to the inside edge of the top plate.

Nail up the second one at the other end of the ridgeboard, and when it is in place, lift the ridgeboard and stand it between the two timbers and

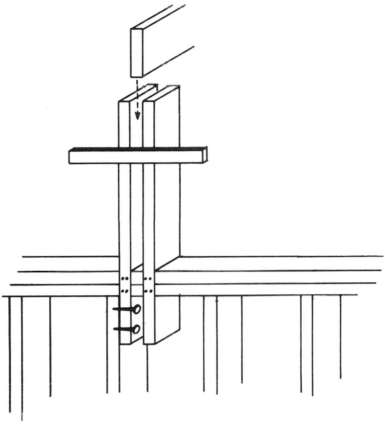

6-1 When installing a ridgeboard single-handedly, construct the device shown here and then lower the end of the ridgeboard into the space where it will be held while the other end is positioned.

let the bottom rest on the crosspiece you nailed in place. The ridgeboard is now in its exact position, and it will remain there as you nail the rafters to it.

Lift the first rafter and let the bird's-mouth cut slip into place over the top cap or plate. Position the end of the rafter against the side or cheek of the ridgeboard, and sink the first nails through the slant cut and into the ridgeboard. You can then nail through the ridgeboard and into the end of the rafter (FIG. 6-2).

Next nail up the rafter for the opposite side. You will not be able to nail through the ridgeboard and into the end of the rafter, but you can nail through the slant cut and then toenail through the side of the rafter and into the ridgeboard.

Now install all of the remaining rafters across the entire roof. When this is done, you are ready to begin bracing. First, take down the ridgeboard raisers and lay them aside. When you need the timbers, remove the cross pieces and use the timbers.

6-2 The end of a stud, the top plate, the top cap, the rafter (with bird's-mouth cut), and the joist all meet at almost the same point.

You can buy preassembled trusses to install instead of cutting and nailing in your own rafter assemblies. These preassembled trusses cost more but will save time. If you are working alone, you will have trouble handling the weight of prebuilt trusses.

BRACING RAFTERS

The rafters are now ready for the installation of the *collar ties*. These are horizontal timbers reaching from one rafter to its opposite. Before nailing in collar ties, decide the amount of drop you want or need. When you have arrived at a decision, make all collar ties the same height and keep them perfectly horizontal. If you later decide to add rooms in the attic, these collar ties will serve as the ceiling joists for your room (FIG. 6-3).

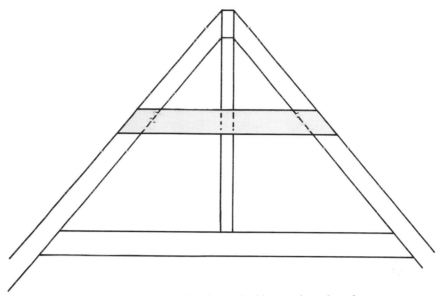

6-3 Collar ties serve as bracing and add strength to the rafters.

There is a formula for calculating the length of collar ties: divide the number of inches in drop by the unit of rise of the common rafter. This figure will equal in feet the distance of one-half of the span. Double the figure and you will have the length of the collar tie.

It is much easier to hold the collar tie in place while marking it for cutting. If you want to drop the collar tie 24 inches from the top of the ridgeboard, mark and measure a 2-foot length of 2 × 4. Cut the timber so that the end is squared, then nail it temporarily to the side of the ridge-board so that it hangs straight down over the center of the building. Be sure to deduct from the vertical piece the width of the collar tie, 3 1/2 inches if you are using 2-×-4 collar ties.

Decide next how to nail the collar tie. There are two basic ways. You can fit the collar tie between the rafters and nail it to the inside or down-side edges of the rafters, or you can nail it to the side or check of the rafter. The second method is favored by many because it provides greater bracing power.

In the first method, the bracing strength of the collar tie is provided only by the nails that extend through the end of the collar tie and into the rafter. The stress will be against the nails as they are sunk into the rafter so that they are parallel with the direction of force. In the second method, the bracing strength is provided by nails driven through the collar tie and into the side of the rafter. Any stress on this brace will be against the nails at right angles.

If you choose to use the second method, hold the collar tie stock so that the top of the stock is firmly and evenly against the bottom edge of the vertical timber you nailed in place against the edge of the ridgeboard. Mark the end of the collar tie at the point where it crosses the outside edge of the rafter. Do this on both sides and saw along the marks. Use the collar tie as a pattern for all future ties you need to install.

If you want the vertical timber to remain at 24 inches, clamp the collar tie stock to the vertical timber so that the bottom of the collar tie stock is flush even with the bottom edge of the vertical timber. Tighten the clamp and the collar tie will be held securely in place while you mark the ends. When you are ready to install the collar ties, all you need to do is start your nails first on both ends, then hold one end in place and nail it so that the outside edges are flush. Drive in only one nail so you can swing the other end slightly for the best fit. Then finish driving all of the nails.

After you cut all of your collar ties according to the pattern you made, take down the vertical timber and save it for later use. If all of your cuts were made properly, the collar ties should all be on the same level, and your ceiling joists for later building are in place.

INSTALLING GUSSETS

Each rafter has three points where additional bracing, called *gusset bracing*, can be installed as protection against the tendency of nails to pull out under stress. Gusset bracing is best made from scraps of plywood.

The first gusset bracing is placed at the point where the ridgeboard meets the rafters. Saw a length of plywood 6 inches wide and long enough to reach across the distance at the ridgeboard. Usually the length needs to be little more than a foot, but you can measure for extra certainty.

Hold the plywood strip so that the top of it is against the bottom of the ridgeboard. Mark along the outside edges of the rafters and saw the plywood in the manner of marking and cutting the collar ties. Cut and install a gusset brace at each rafter juncture (FIG. 6-4).

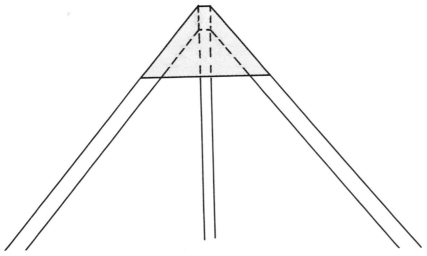

6-4 A type of gusset bracing. The shaded section shows plywood fitted and nailed to rafters and ridgeboard supports.

Now mark and cut a similar section of plywood where the top cap or plate meets the rafters. Hold the plywood for marking so that the end of the plywood is in line with the inside edge of the top cap or plate. Mark along the upper edge of the rafter and the bottom edge of the joists (FIG. 6-5). Cut the gusset along the marks and nail it in place. Do the same on the other side of the building.

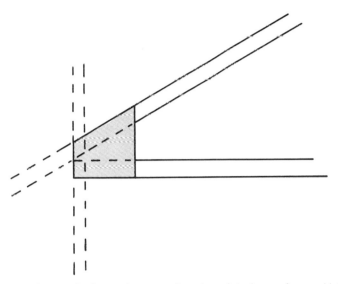

6-5 Gusset bracing can also be used to strengthen the point where rafters and joists meet.

When the gussets are installed at these three points, you have prevented separation of the roof at these points. The use of gussets requires very little plywood, and the degree of protection makes the investment a great bargain. The major protection is against the possibility that you were sold lumber that was not fully cured. When a nail is sunk into a timber, the nail forces the fibers of the wood apart. The nail remains in place because of the intense pressure of the wood against the shank of the nail. As long as that pressure is very firm, the nail will hold. If the pressure is released or lessened, the nail becomes loose.

Green lumber or lumber with a high moisture content will provide adequate pressure when the nail is first driven. However, when the moisture evaporates from the wood, the fibers shrink, and the nail is not surrounded by the same intense pressure. The result is that the nail becomes extremely loose and finally will not hold at all.

Also, as the moisture content is decreased, the wood tends to curve and bow. If there is the pressure of weight above the wood, the wood will bow in the direction of the force of the weight. This bowing will cause the ends to turn upward, which will cause nails to work out even farther.

Eventually the nails barely hold, and the house is weakened drastically. The obvious solution is to buy and install only well-cured lumber. The problem is that when you buy from the lumber yard, you are sold what is in stock—and stock lumber might or might not be well-cured. This is why you should install these gussets and other supports. While the extra time, effort, and money might not seem necessary at the time you are building, the positive effects of good bracing might not even be visible. You will, however, clearly see the negative effects of not bracing well when you are building.

After you have installed collar tie braces, gussets at the ridgeboard and at the plates, your individual trusses are fairly well supported against all but the heaviest snowstorms or highest winds. You can now add rafter/joist supports for the final bracing of trusses.

INSTALLING RAFTER/JOIST SUPPORTS

When you installed the collar tie braces, you spaced and nailed them in so that the braces could serve as ceiling joists for a room, if you choose later to add living space in the attic. The rafter/joist supports can serve a similar purpose. They can become the studding of the wall frames of the rooms in the attic, if you elect to convert the attic into rooms.

These 2-×-4 timbers can be installed with the top ends nailed securely to the rafters and the bottom ends nailed to the ceiling joists for the rooms below. If you want to do so, you can test the rafter height at various points in the attic to see if the roof will be high enough to serve as a room. Directly under the ridgeboard the height will probably be sufficient, but as the roof slopes downward, you lose height rapidly.

Even if the roof is not high enough for you to stand upright as you move away from the ridgeboard area, you might still want to consider the possibility of adding rooms in the attic. Beds and various items of furniture can be positioned against the walls and leave the center area free for movement. If the main part of your house is 20 feet from plate to plate, you will probably have at least a width of 10 to 12 feet of usable attic space. Consider that many rooms in conventional homes are no more than 12 feet wide. It is logical that if you plan to support the rafters anyway, you might as well install the supports so that they can be of later service should you eventually choose to add a room or two upstairs.

Measure from the center of the house to the extreme points of useful space. Then measure the height of the room from the top of the ceiling joists to the bottom of the rafters.

To cut the rafter/joist supports, you will need to cut one square end and one slanted end. Hold the timber you plan to use so that the square end rests on the top edge of the ceiling joist. Let the top end of the timber extend past the bottom edge of the rafter so you can mark for the slant cut. You need to hold the timber perfectly vertical in order to make the proper marks. You can hold the level against the timber with one hand and with the other hand mark the cut line.

When the timber is cut and you are ready to install, stand it so that it fits snugly into position. Start nailing the slant cut by sinking two nails through the slant and into the rafter. Then toenail the bottom end to the top of the joist. If you have trouble holding the timber in place while you nail, find a scrap piece of lumber (almost anything will do, from a short 2 × 4 to an end of a 1-×-5 board or piece of plywood) and nail it temporarily to the top of the joist. Locate it so that the front edge of the scrap lumber is on the line where the back of the support timber will be nailed.

When you start to nail, the scotch piece will prevent the timber from slipping backward and you can nail easily. When you have completed nailing, remove the scotch scrap and use it on the next timber.

One handy step is to install the first and last support timbers and then to run a chalk line from the first to the last so that you will be certain of keeping your wall line straight. Later if you choose to install wall covers, you will have straight, well-spaced nailing surfaces ready.

If you wish to add additional bracing, use shorter scraps of lumber and install diagonal braces from the bottom of the rafter/joist brace to the rafter itself. Let the angle of the brace dissect the distance between the plate and the rafter/joist brace you have just installed.

SHED ROOF BRACING

A shed roof is the easiest of any roof to install, which is why it was not covered in the previous chapter. Such a roof is made up of one slope or pitch and may be thought of as one-half of a gable roof. The common rafter, which will be the only type used in the shed roof (unless you desire to install a shed dormer, which is unlikely), runs from the plate of the front to the plate of the back. Each common rafter will have two bird's-mouth cuts so that it will fit snugly and well over the plates.

Space the common rafters as you would in any other type of roof. Use 16-inch centers and you can use solid bridging between the rafters.

The majority of the bracing, in addition to bridging, will be in the wall frames. Run diagonal braces from the plate to the corner post, and have supports between the common rafter and the top of the plate. These support pieces will be very short, but should be installed as you would install studs or cripple studs.

In the shed roof you have no ridgeboard. If you wish to add a shed dormer, you can do so by omitting the common rafters where the dormer will be added and installing upper and lower headers—just as you did for other dormers or gables. Then add the cripple rafters above and below the dormer.

Dormer rafters will have one plumb cut and one angle cut. The angle cut is so that the rafter will lie smoothly against the cripple rafters above the upper header. Nail the slant cut ends of the rafter in position. Extend the rafters to the desired lengths and support them with a plate, under which you nail the studding or bracing on each side of the dormer.

INSTALLING ROOF SHEATHING

You can cover the rafter with some form of sheathing (often pronounced ''sheeting''), which is the first or lowest roof covering you will install. This sheathing is, like subflooring, a vital part of the framing of a house.

The sheathing strengthens the roof, in addition to adding insulation and protection against roof damage in stormy weather.

Many years ago board sheathing was used, either tongue-and-groove or straight-edge lumber. The boards were nailed on each rafter and ends were staggered so that no two successive courses of boards ended on the same rafter.

In modern building plywood sheathing is used almost universally. There are several good reasons. A panel of plywood is 4 feet wide and 8 feet long. One man working alone can cover 32 square feet in a matter of minutes. Because of the speed of installation, plywood is very inexpensive compared to board sheathing. Plywood is also extremely strong and durable. It offers great stability to a roof, and there are few if any weak places where breakage will likely occur. Yet another great advantage of plywood is that you can nail very near the edges without worrying about splitting. This is not true of boards. Nearly all pine boards will start to split if you drive a nail within 1 inch of the end of the board, unless the nail is very small.

When you are using boards for sheathing, it will be necessary for board ends to meet on top of rafters. The top edge of a rafter is about $1^3/4$ inches wide at most, which means that at every end of a board you will be likely to cause splitting when you drive a nail into the board end.

If you happen to have a great deal of sheathing lumber handy and want to use it, you can do so if you will follow a few basic operations. First, use only very sound timbers. If there is a weak area—a loose knot or knot hole, or softening wood—do not use the timber. If necessary, you can save it and use it by cutting sections of it to fill in at the ends of courses.

When you are sawing boards, try to mark off your line cuts so that you can miss knots. These knots will often break away from the board and leave weak ends. Worse, it is difficult to drive a nail through knots. You will either bend the nail or you will cause the knot to shatter, or both.

When you are nailing board ends on top of a rafter, move the point of the nail back an inch or so from the usual nailing spot and angle-nail into the rafter. By doing so you will keep from splitting the end of the board and you will strengthen the board end. When you end boards on a rafter, cut each board end so that the space atop the rafter is evenly divided. Otherwise you will have too little room for nailing.

If you cannot avoid leaving narrow nailing spaces, you can always nail a short 2 × 4 against the side of the rafter so that you have adequate nailing surface. Do not allow the added 2 × 4 to extend past the upper edge of the rafter. If you do, your shingles will not lie flat and you will run a greater risk of damage during storms.

Start at the eaves or overhangs of the roof area and nail in the first board so that the outer edge of the board is even with the edge of the rafters. Check each rafter for proper alignment.

If you prefer board sheathing, you can sometimes find rough-cut 1-×-4 or 1-×-5 boards that are much cheaper than finished lumber. The rough-cut boards are actually stronger than the finished lumber because during finishing the planer cuts away all of the rougher areas and a 1-×-5 board usually ends up measuring 5/8 by 4 1/2. The rough cut lumber can be very rough to handle, but the boards are strong and highly serviceable. This lumber also does not have a nice appearance, but it will not be seen, except from the attic, once the shingles are installed.

After you install the first board, push each succeeding board tightly against the previous one as you proceed to work your way up the roof line. Use two 8-penny nails each place the boards cross a rafter.

Years ago builders installed board sheathing diagonally rather than at right angles to the rafters. This type of sheathing installation creates a stronger framing effect, but it slows down the work because of the time it takes to make the angle cuts. An angle cut is, by necessity, longer than a right-angle cut and will take more sawing time and effort, particularly if you are working without a power saw.

When you install plywood sheathing, decide first what thickness of plywood to buy. The thicker the panel, the more it will cost. The 5/8-inch panels are extremely strong and durable and make fine sheathing. If you use the very thin panels you will find slight sagging between rafters. If you ever need to walk across the shingled roof to make repairs or for other reasons, you will be able to feel the thin sheathing sink or give slightly as you cross it.

Whatever thickness you use, nail it with 8-penny nails spaced a foot apart on every rafter. Do not try to be economical with nails at the expense of poor security in the nailing. Nails can be bought for less than $1 per pound, and you will use a surprisingly small amount of nails in an entire roof.

Start at the eaves end of one slope of the framed roof and position the first panel of plywood in the corner. One edge should extend 1 inch over the rafter ends, with the other edge even with the outside edge of the last rafter. Before you sink any nails, check to see that the inside edge of the plywood rests about one-half the way across the final rafter where it will be nailed.

If you do not have adequate nailing room for the next panel that will abut the one you have laid out, you will need to make necessary adjustments. Here is one of the crucial areas of your work. If rafters were laid out properly, you will have a perfect fit for the 4-foot-wide panels. If not, panels will have to be modified.

One of the best ways to handle plywood is to lay panels across the joists for the ceiling so that you can stand on these while you attempt to move the plywood into its correct position. Lay the support panels in the far corner of the house framing, as near as possible to the place where you are working.

Lay the first panel of plywood out so that it will reach across as many rafters as possible. When in position, it should cover the end rafter and two other rafters before ending halfway across the fourth rafter. By laying it out in this manner, you are tying together or reinforcing as many rafters as possible for maximum strength against wind.

You can nail the upper edges of the panel, but you will not be able to reach across the entire 4-foot expanse of plywood. You will have to lean across the plywood in order to nail. While this work is not dangerous in the real sense of the word, do not be careless and risk injury by falling.

Before attempting to nail the bottom edge of the plywood, be sure to nail down the near edges carefully so that there is no danger that the panel will slide. Avoid sheathing a roof in high winds, because the wind can lift the panel and actually blow it from the roof.

Start the nailing by sinking one nail in the corner where the final outside rafter and the plywood are aligned. Drive the nail in far enough to hold the corner in place but do not sink it completely, in case you will have to move it to make minor placement adjustments.

When the first nail is holding, recheck the alignment of the remainder of the panel. You will need to move around the end of the panel so that you can see if it aligns well with the plumb cut ends of the rafter extensions.

If all is as it should be, sink a nail near the edge of the plywood nearest the peak of the roof and drive it in all the way. Then finish sinking the first nail you started. The plywood is now anchored at two points and cannot shift appreciably.

Drive nails 1 inch from the edge and into the rafters until you have firmly anchored the top side of the panel. Then move down the panel 1 foot and sink another row of nails. Repeat this pattern until the entire panel is firmly nailed in place.

Lay the next panel so that the 4-foot end abuts the end of the first panel. Again, align the entire panel, sink the holding nail partially, and recheck. If the panel is in place, complete nailing as you did earlier.

Complete the entire row of panels until you have covered the final 4 feet of the first roof slope. When the section is completed, move your support panels across the joists and nail in the second row of panels. You will find that the work moves very rapidly and efficiently if rafter alignment is correct.

You can buy grooved decking nails for use with plywood, if you want to use these. These special nails which cost more than $1 per pound are therefore slightly more expensive than wire nails. Many people believe they are worth the extra money because they will not pull out under stress and bucking over the years.

The only difficulty with the special grooved nails is that they have a slender shank that is made even more fragile by the grooves, and the nails tend to bend easily if they are not driven perfectly straight. If one starts to bend and you attempt to realign it by tapping it with a hammer or by using the claws to straighten the nail, the nail will snap in half. This is not common but it does happen. You can have the nail heads break away from the shank while you are driving.

As you move higher up the roof slope, you will find that you need a ladder or scaffolding on which to stand while you work. A step ladder resting upon plywood panels over joists is not a particularly safe arrangement. If you choose to do this, be sure that the ends of the panel are resting solidly upon the ceiling joists. If one end extends a foot or more unsupported and you step on that end, the panel end might sink and create a very dangerous situation.

One solution is to turn the panel at a slight angle so that both ends are well supported by the joists. You might also wish to use saw horses with long timbers across them and a panel of plywood over the boards. The arrangement will provide you with a sturdy working base.

Many workers climb out onto the plywood to do the nailing. Usually the panels are not slippery, but wear soft-soled shoes for maximum traction. Be advised that you can very easily slip and fall, so use great caution while you are in such a position.

When one slope is completed up to the ridgeboard, let the edge of the sheathing panel extend slightly beyond the edge so that the next panel that abuts it will actually lie across the end of the previous panel. The lap will provide a near-perfect seal for the two panels.

Start the next slope when the first is completed. You will have little choice at this point but to climb out onto the roof after you have nailed the first few rows of panels into place. If you are working alone, be sure to locate a long ladder at the eaves for your descent, and when you have sheathed a large portion of the roof, count the number of panels you will need to complete the job and haul these out onto the sheathed part of the roof.

When the slope is nearly completed, position the final panel at the ridgeboard to see if it will fit well. Check the lap seal at the top. Then nail in the panels along the ridgeboard.

If you have a basic gable roof with two gentle slopes, your work here is finished. You will need to apply the final roofing materials as quickly as possible, because the plywood panels will not prevent leaks and water damage. It is a good idea to listen to weather forecasts, particularly during unsettled times of the year, before you begin this phase of your work. Try to avoid getting started with the sheathing, then having to wait for days while a storm center lingers over your area.

As soon as possible, then, apply the final roofing materials and "dry in" the house. Afterwards, store all building materials that can be damaged by water under the roof.

If you have dormers or unusual roof angles and slopes to sheath, you will need to complete work on these after the basic slopes have been covered. Sheath these dormers exactly as you did the remainder of the roof.

Mark the cut lines by leaning a panel of plywood in place and marking it along the ridgeboard or studding. Cut and install the sections as before.

Some builders use plywood as boxing to close in the ends of the rafters. Other prefer wide boards, and still others have a variety of preferences. Whatever you use, this is one of the most difficult and precarious jobs you will face. Use utmost care while performing the work.

You will need to work from a ladder or scaffolding, and while ladder work at such a height is disconcerting, it is also very difficult to rig scaffolding high enough to accomplish the work. If you are working alone, start a nail in the boxing material so that the nail will hit the end rafter end and one other rafter end.

Earlier you left 1 inch of plywood extending past the plumb-cut ends of the rafters and another inch extending past the outside edge of the final rafter on each side of the roof. That spare inch was to allow for boxing to be installed. You could, if you neglected to leave the inch, install the boxing so that it laps the ends of the plywood. The major disadvantage here is that you have a crack exposed to the elements before you can install final roofing. With blowing rains, you might even have this problem after the roof is installed.

If you left the inch, measure, mark, and cut the boxing materials and sink two nails partially—just until the point penetrates the material. When you are ready to install the boards, climb to your work place and hold the boxing in place with one hand while you drive one of the started nails into the ends of the rafters. When the first nail is secured, drive the second nail. The boxing will remain in place while you complete the nailing.

You will find that the installation of boxing is far easier if you have help. It is very difficult to hold one end of a long board while you nail the other end. Unless you have considerable strength in your forearms, or unless you have help, you will find the job both taxing and dangerous.

If you have no help, you can make a simple device which will help to hold the boxing while you nail it. Use a scrap of 1-x-4 board about 18 inches long, although length is not a primary consideration. Even with one end nail two strips of similar board material about 4 inches wide. Nail one on top of the other and flat against the longer board. Then use a piece of similar board about 6 or 7 inches long so that there is a gap between the doubled boards and the other two boards. Nail the assembly into the edge of the plywood sheathing so that the gap is positioned with the bottom of the gap about even with the bottom edge of the rafter.

When you are ready to work, slide one end of the boxing material through the gap and the assembly will hold one end of the boxing firmly in place while you adjust and nail the other end. Nail the boxing to three or four rafter ends before you remove the assembly and nail the free end. The sheathing is completed.

Chapter **7**

Stairways

*W*hen you contemplate stairway construction, there are many choices to make. First you can decide whether to buy the stairway as a unit assembly or to construct your own. If you choose to build your own, you have many additional choices available to you.

One of the first considerations is how the stairs will be used, aside from the obvious functions. Will the stairway be simply utilitarian or will it also be decorative? Will the stairs be located in the center of the home or will they be concealed in an out-of-the-way area? You can have circular stairways if your space is limited; or long, curving stairs; or you can settle for the straight ascent types with little or no landings at the top.

Stairways are costly to install. The longer the stairway and the more decorative you choose to make it, the greater the expense is likely to be. There are many types of materials, and these vary widely in cost. Oak is much more expensive than pine, and there are several grades of lumber available in most types of wood.

Some stairways are intended for the sole purpose of allowing residents of the house to climb from one floor to another with a minimum of difficulty. Others are sweeping, wide enough for three or four people to walk abreast, and elaborately decorated. If you are building your own house, largely to save money, you will probably not be interested in the more lavish types of stairways, but will prefer to remain close to the basic concepts.

A DESCRIPTION OF TERMS

Most stairs have several basic components. The *treads* are the actual portions of the stairways that people step upon while they are climbing stairs. The *stringers* are the long running boards or timbers that support the treads. Stringers are important because they contain the entire weight of the stairway if there is not a solid support built in underneath. Stringers, as mentioned earlier, are also called strings, horses, and carriages (FIG. 7-1).

The support strip under the tread is called the *cleat*. It is possible to construct very serviceable stairways that contain only stringers, treads, and cleats (FIG. 7-2).

The remainder of the typical stairway consists of the *risers*, which are the backs of the treads that fill in between one tread and another, the

7-1   This stairway, seen from the underside, is supported by three stringers, the strongest in the center.

nosing, which is the portion of the tread that extends slightly past the riser, the *floor line*, which is the point where the stairs terminate at the bottom, and the *stairwell header*, where the top of the stairs is connected to the second floor. The *rail* or railing is the handgrip located against a

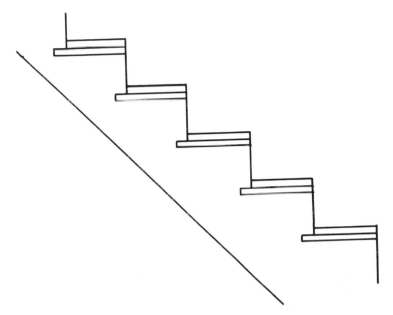

7-2 Treads with the cleats installed under the treads. Usually cleats are used only with stringers that do not have cutouts for treads.

wall or at the end of treads and at a height of about 36 inches. The rails provide added support for the climbers on the stairs.

The *unit rise* is the amount of ascent for each riser. If the difference between steps or treads is 8 inches, then you have a unit rise of 8 inches. The width of each tread or step is called the *unit run*. If steps or treads are a foot deep, you have a unit run of 12 inches. The complete distance from one floor to the termination point of the stairway is called the *total rise*. The distance covered on a horizontal plane from the first step to the last is called the *total run* (FIG. 7-3).

It is possible to have a total run of stairs that amounts to only 5 or 6 feet and yet have a total rise of 10 or 12 feet. Such stairways are unusually steep or precipitous and can be dangerous.

It is also possible to have a total run of 10 feet or more and a total rise of only 5 or 6 feet. The unit run and the total run, as well as the unit rise and the total rise, depend almost entirely on the purpose and function of the stairs. Calculate your own unit and total rise and run in terms of the space you have available and the utilitarian needs to be met by the stairs.

CONSTRUCTING A SIMPLE STAIRWAY

A stringer and tread stairway can be built by using only two wide boards for stringers, a number of shorter wide boards for treads, and a series of thin cleats or supports under both ends of all treads. You will also need bracing or headers. If the total run is very long (more than 12 feet) you will need supports under the stringers, particularly if the stairs are to be used for transporting heavy materials or a number of heavy people.

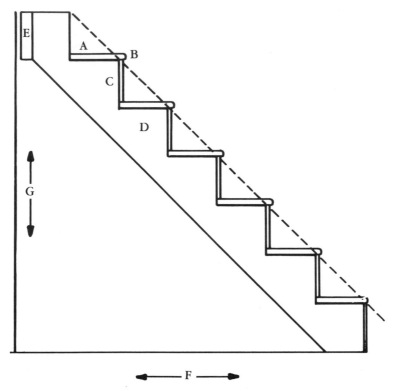

7-3 The vital elements of a stairway: (A) the tread, (B) the nosing, (C) the riser, (D) the stringer, (E) the header, (F) total run, and (G) total rise.

Calculating rise and run

To build the simple stairway, first calculate the total rise and total run of the stairs. Remember, the total rise is the complete vertical distance from the floor to the top of the stairs that will be covered by the stairway.

Decide where you want the stairs to be located. Build and install the stairs after the subflooring has been installed but before the finished flooring is in place.

Start by dropping a plumb line from the top of the stairway location to the floor beneath. You can use a plumb bob or you can use a long timber and a level. If you use a plumb bob, attach the string to the edge of the joist on the second floor. Then allow the weighted end to descend slowly until it is only a fraction of an inch from the subflooring below. Wait until the weight has stopped swinging before you mark the vertical descent point.

When the descent point is marked, use your carpenter's square to lay off the stairway width at perfect right angles to the wall framing. Then measure from the line you have made to the point where the stairway ascent will start. This distance is the total run.

If you are using a timber and a level, stand the timber so that it is perfectly vertical. Hold the level against the side of the timber to assure yourself of a vertical reading. Mark the floor at the back side of the timber, not on the front: The front will be almost 4 inches out of plumb because of the thickness of the timber.

Now determine the precise total rise of the stairs. If you are using traditional ceiling heights, the rise will be 8 feet. If you are using variant heights, measure to be sure of the total rise.

The next step is to decide the height of the unit rise and the width or depth of the unit run. If you have room for only a run of 8 feet, divide 96 inches by the height you wish to have for each tread. Many people prefer a unit rise of 7 inches, so divide 7 into 96 (12 × 8—the vertical rise and the inches in a foot). Note: You will not be concerned with the fractional remainder of the figure you reach. The figure represents the number of risers you will have, and you cannot have a fractional number. You may, if the fractional remainder nearly equals a whole, decide to move up to the next number.

In this case the number of risers is 13.7. Either round it off at 13 or increase it to 14. If you round it off at 13, you will have to install risers that are slightly higher than the traditional 7-inch graduations. If you raise the number of risers to 14, you will need longer total run distance or you will have to make the stairway steeper.

If you don't mind an added inch of riser height, a simple solution would be to increase the risers to 8 inches and have 12 of them. By doing so you could actually reduce the total run distance as you reduce the number of risers. The only real problem would be the use of the steps. Most people over the years have gotten accustomed to 7-inch risers, and any amount more or less than that distance might cause accidents.

Stringers

When you decide upon your riser height and the number of risers—which is largely determined by the total rise and total run distances—choose the stringers. These are the lengthy timbers that will support the treads. You will need a plumb cut at the top where the stringers will be attached to the headers. You will also need a horizontal cut at the bottom where the stringers will rest upon the floor.

To make the plumb cut, choose stringers that are long enough to reach from the header, sometimes called the "well header," where the stairs will be fastened to the upper floor framing, and to the anchor point, which is where the bottom ends of the stringers will be fastened in place. Following is a formula that will help you to calculate the length needed for stringers.

Think of the area to be serviced by the stairs as a triangle, with the vertical distance or total rise as one side, the total run as another side, and the stringers as the third side or hypotenuse of the triangle. Determine the hypotenuse of the triangle by squaring the distances representing the total rise and the total run, then adding the squares. Then take the square root of the total.

For instance, if the total rise or vertical distance from the bottom floor to the subflooring above is 8 feet, square that figure. The result is 64. If the total run or horizontal distance is 13 feet, square that number. The result is 169. Now add the two figures and the sum is 233. Now figure the square root of 233, which is 15.264337—rounded off to 15.3. That means that your stringer will need to be 15 feet and 4 inches.

Select stringer stock now. The timbers should be no smaller than 2 × 6 and should be, if available, 2 × 8 or larger.

You are ready to make the plumb cut and the horizontal or anchor cut on the stringers. The simple way is to lean the stringer timber in its correct position and use a level to help you decide on where to mark it. If you need to, you can set the stringer in place and mark the vertical and horizontal cuts. The anchor point of the stringer will be sitting on the corner of the timber, and the header end will be sitting on the bottom edge of the stringer. Both of these heights are slightly incorrect, but the discrepancies will not be great.

To mark more accurately, lay a short length of 2 × 4 under each end of the stringer. On the top end hold a level so that it is flush against the header and so the side is against the stringer. When the bubble is centered, mark along the level so that the mark is on the inside edge of the level. In this instance the inside edge will be the edge that is nearer the anchor point. Leave the stringer in place and go down to the other end. Lay the level across the 2 × 4 so that it dissects the lower part of the stringer. Center the bubble and mark along the top edge of the level. This line will be the horizontal cut line.

You will not have perfect cut lines if you use this method, but you will be so close the inaccuracy will be negligible. You will have accurate plumb and horizontal lines, and any inaccuracy will be in the actual length of the stringer. The degree of error will be less than 1 inch.

For an even more precise method of marking the stringer, use your carpenter's square. Lay the stringer on its side and hold the square with the tongue in your right hand and the blade in your left hand. The tongue is the shorter part of the square. The heel, or corner, of the square should be pointed away from your body.

Move to the end of the stringer and lay the square on it so that the tongue is roughly parallel to the point on the stringer end that will leave you the approximate desired cut. Set the square tongue on the unit run, which will be the depth of your steps. If you want steps 10 inches wide, set the unit run on the 10 marking. Set the blade on the unit rise mark. If your steps are to be 7 inches high, set the blade on 7.

Mark along the outside edge of the square and continue the cut line all the way to the opposite edge of the stringer so that you will have marked a triangle off. Cut along the line. This will be the bottom of the stair, and the cut edge should sit flatly and evenly on the subflooring or other surface at the bottom of the stairs.

Now make the plumb or vertical cut. Set the stringer so that the anchor point is in position and the top of the stringer sits on the joist or header. Mark according to a center bubble reading. If you want to mark and cut without having to use the stringer in position, use the carpenter's square again.

Hold the square as you did earlier, tongue in right hand and blade in left, and lay it as close to the end of the stringer as you can and still have marking room. Set the tongue on the unit rise and the blade on the length. Mark along the square and saw. If you set the square properly, the cut line should be perfectly plumb and should fit against the header easily.

If the header is not yet in position, you should install it at this point. Use a length of timber that is as long as the stair opening and as wide as the joist against which it will be nailed. It is better if the header can be slightly wider than the timber from which you cut the stringers, because the angle cut on the end of the stringer will be seated against the header.

Use at least three rows of three nails each, driven through the header and into the joist. Use 16-penny nails for sufficient holding strength. If the nails extend through the joist, bend the nails so that they cannot work free in the coming weeks and months when pressure is exerted on the stairway.

There is an old carpentry term called *clinching*. The term means to bend the final fraction of an inch of a nail that is driven. The purpose of clinching is to prevent nails from working free. Not many builders clinch nails in our era, but if you wish to use this ancient method, you will practically guarantee yourself that the nails into the header will not work free at either end.

When you are ready to attach the first stringer, stand it in position. Be sure that the plumb cut fits well against the header, and that the horizontal cut seats evenly on the subfloor or other surface at the bottom. If the stringer fits precisely, use it as a pattern to mark the other stringer.

Place the stringer in position for nailing at this time and toenail it to the header. Use at least three 16-penny nails that are spaced across the stringer, but not close enough to the edge to split the wood. If there is room, toenail from both sides of the stringer.

Nail in the second stringer. Space it so that there is barely sufficient room between the two stringers for the treads to fit later. If there is room below the stringer, you can nail in a support strip. Use 2-×-4 or 2-×-2 lumber and fit the strip under the stringers. Nail the strip to the header. Now the stringers and the stairway will have the support of the nails as well as the strip under the stringers.

At the bottom or anchor end, toenail the other end of the stringers to the subflooring. Again, use three 16-penny nails on each stringer.

Now you are ready to install the treads. Choose tread stock with care. In this very simple stairway there will be no supports under the treads except for cleats at each end. If the stairs must support very heavy people or objects, the treads must be durable and strong enough not to weaken, give, or break.

Use 2-×-6 or 2-×-8 treads if the stock is available. Measure and mark the cut line for the first tread. After you saw the tread, check it for fit. You want it to fit snugly but not so tightly that it forces the stringers apart. You have a good fit when you can slip the tread into position without having to hammer or otherwise force it into place. When you have a good fit, use the first tread as a pattern and cut all others accordingly. Try to cut so that the cut line will be eliminated by the saw blade.

Mark the stringers where the treads are to be installed. Use your level to lay out the installation marks. Measure up from the subflooring 7 inches from the outside edge of the stringers. Mark the points on both stringers. Then place the level so that the mark is even with the top edge of the level and the bubble is centered. Mark across the stringer. This is where the top edge of the tread will be located.

Treads and cleats

To install treads, hold the tread in position and drive three 16-penny nails through the outside of the stringer and into the ends of the treads. Do this on both sides. Then add the cleats.

Cleats are support strips, usually of 2-×-2 stock, nailed or bolted into place under the treads. Do not neglect this extra step. Nails are only lengths of wire with a head. Wire bends very easily under pressure. If you omit to add the cleats, each time someone climbs the stairs there will be pressure on the wires or nails. After a period of time the nails might start to bend. When they bend sufficiently, they will slip from the ends of the treads and subject the climber to possibly serious injury.

Cut the 2-×-2 strips the same length as the width of the treads, or slightly shorter. You can drive nails through the stringer and into the cleats, as you did the treads, but it is very effective to drive through the cleats and into the stringer also. If the nails stick out the other side of the stringer, use a hacksaw and saw off the nails. Use at least three nails in each tread. Do not drive close to the edge. If you split the wood, nearly all of the holding power is destroyed.

The best possible way to install the cleats is to use a drill and bolts. Drill two holes through the stringer and also through the cleats. Run the bolts through the holes so that the heads of the bolts are on the outside of the stringers. Add washers on the end of the bolts and add nuts. Tighten securely.

At this point your basic stairway is complete and ready to use. Such stairs are well suited for entry into basements, work shops, and similar locations, but are not particularly suited for the more formal parts of the house (FIG. 7-4).

BUILDING RUSTIC STAIRS

If you are building a second home, cabin, or other rustic dwelling, you might want to consider adding a rustic stairway to the house or cabin. These stairs consist of two small logs and treads. That is all. But the stairs are very strong, easy to make, and inexpensive.

Start with the logs. These can be pine, poplar, or any other straight-trunked tree. The logs should actually be the trunks of trees that are slightly larger than saplings, because they usually do not have to support a

7-4 This basic stairway is easy and inexpensive to build.

great amount of weight. Larger logs are too heavy for one person to handle.

Stringers

To make the stairs, start with the stringers, which in this case will be the logs. Calculate your length before you begin work. Remember to square your vertical height, which for purposes of illustration will be 10 feet. The first step is to square the figure, which gives you 100. Next, decide upon the total run or horizontal distance to be covered by the stairs. Assume that the total run is 15 feet. Square this figure and you have 225. Add 225 and 100 and you have 325.

The third side or hypotenuse is the distance you need to reach. To find it, take the square root of 325. The figure is 18.02, but you can round off to 18. You will now need two logs 18 feet long. The logs can be 6 inches in diameter at their largest.

Remove the bark from the logs, which should be as free of knots and other irregularities as possible. You can use a mattock to strip away the bark, or if you are using poplar you can let the log lie in the sun for a few days and the bark will pop off the trunk easily.

If you don't want to use logs, use larger timbers such as 6 × 6. You can buy this type of timber at most lumber yards. The timber itself can be dressed into a beautiful piece of lumber that will be aesthetically desirable in almost any home.

Decide on the type of stringers you wish to use and locate the stringer stock. Also decide on the number of risers or treads you will have and how high each tread should be above the previous one. Now you are ready to mark off the tread locations and install the treads.

Treads

You will need to install the treads into the actual body of the stringers rather than use cleats solely for added support. Use a level to get the right markings for cuts. When you have marked the log or beam, use a handsaw, crosscut saw, or even chain saw to make the cuts.

For each tread you will need to make four cuts. The first cut is where the bottom of the tread will rest. The second cut on each stringer location will represent the top of the tread. The two cuts should be about 2 inches apart. Next use a chisel to knock out the wood between the two cuts. The cuts should be about 2 inches deep, no more. Make the cuts and chisel out the wood on both sides of the stringers. Then cut your treads and insert these into the slots you have made. You will probably have to slide the treads in from the front (FIG. 7-5).

When treads are in place, use 16-penny nails to nail through the side of the log and into the end of the treads. The slots you cut will be the bottom supports for the treads. The nails are mainly to keep the treads from moving inside the slot. If you wish, you can drive nails at an angle up through the bottom of the treads and into the log that serves as a stringer.

Be sure to test logs for moisture content. When you lift the log, it should not be abnormally heavy, unless you are using such wood as oak or locust. Second, when you drive a nail, there should not be sap or other moisture forming around the point of entry. Third, when you need to pull out a nail, if it slips out easily, the wood is either moisture-laden or too soft to be useful in building.

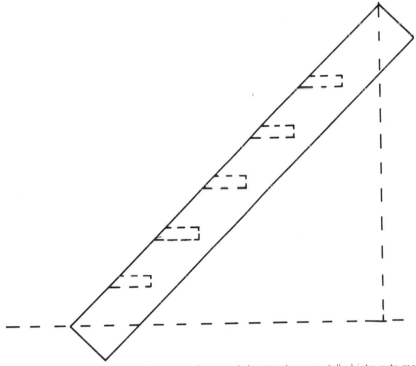

7-5 In a rustic stairway the stringers are logs, and the treads are installed into cuts made into the logs.

Bracing

You can brace either of the types of stairs listed here by cutting support posts and installing these under the stairs. The log stairs probably will not need to be braced at all, but you might wish to install 2-×-4 bracing at the halfway point in the first stairs described. You can also install bracing at the one-third and two-third points.

To brace, stand a length of 2-×-4 so that one end is on the subflooring and the other is against the side or cheek of the stringer. Hold a level against the brace piece so that you get a vertical reading, then mark the brace timber where it crosses the bottom of the stringer. Cut along the mark and install. Fit the slant cut under the stringer and nail up through the cut and into the stringer. Use two 16-penny nails.

Nail the other end to the subflooring or to a runner of 2-×-4 timber, if you plan to frame in around the stairway. This runner serves as a sole plate for the closet studding, if you choose to add a closet or storage space here.

Install the braces on both stringers. If you later decide to add the closet space, you can add other brace pieces and let these serve also as studding.

To brace the rustic stairs—if you feel that you should—use short lengths of the same materials you used for stringers. If you use 6-×-6 beams, one support on each side of the stringers at the halfway point should be sufficient. If you are using log supports, choose a length that is basically the same diameter as that used in the stringer and use one on each side of the stringers at the halfway points.

USING CUTOUT STRINGERS

Cutout stringers are one of the most popular types of stairway framing. They differ from common stringers in that they have the spaces for the treads cut out. When you use cutout stringers you do not use cleats.

You can use three rather than two stringers (or more, if the situation warrants) when you use cutout stringers. The added stringer in the center adds enough support that you do not have to worry as much about thickness of treads.

Marking the cutout stringer can be a rather confusing bit of work. Following are instructions on how to mark the cutout stringer at the top, the anchor point end, and all the treads along the stringers.

Here, as in all stairway construction, you must calculate the length of the stringers. Again, you will use the squares of the two numbers representing the total rise and total run. Add the numbers and take the square root, which will give you the total distance or length of the stringers.

Measure and mark carefully. You will be using 2-×-10 or 2-×-12 stock, which are both very expensive. You do not want to ruin a piece of such valuable lumber.

Start by laying the stringer stock flat across a pair of sawhorses. Use the carpenter's square to find the proper marking points. Hold the tongue of the square in the right hand and the blade in the left, with the heel pointing away from the body.

Set the square to the unit run on the tongue. The unit run is the horizontal distance covered by each tread. If the tread is to be 12 inches deep, the unit run is 12. The total run is the complete distance covered by the stairs.

Set the blade to the unit rise. The total rise is the vertical distance from floor to the next floor, but the unit rise is the height of each riser. If the height of each riser is 7 inches, set the blade on 7.

You now have the tongue set at 12 and the blade set to 7. Mark from the point where the blade crosses the stringer to the heel of the square. At the heel, mark along the square as the blade moves at a right angle to the mark you just made. Mark along the blade until it runs off the stringer.

The long mark will become the tread for the stringer, and the short mark will mark the riser. Mark the next tread and riser by placing the square—using the same settings—at the exact point where the previous mark left the stringer. Mark along the tongue and blade as before, and the second tread and riser is marked. Hold the square firmly in place while you mark. Continue this process until you have marked all of the treads and risers for the stringer. Then hold the stringer in position to make a visual check for the basic accuracy of the marks.

When you are satisfied with the markings, cut out for the treads and risers. You can install the stringers by nailing a length of lumber across the rough opening if you have not done so already. This timber is the header for the opening. It should measure at least 2 × 6 and there should be enough room for the ends of the stringers to rest securely on the top of the header timber—just as a notched joist rests atop a girder or ledger plate.

Fasten the stringers on each side of the stairway to the rough opening framing. You can use nails, but bolts, while more expensive, provide greater support. You can use both nails and bolts if you want double support.

Drill a hole from the inside edge of the stringer through the timber for the rough framing. Then run a bolt through the hole, and on the other end use a metal washer and nut. Tighten the nut until the washer starts to embed slightly into the framing timber. Repeat this process until you have two bolts (or three, if you feel it necessary) in each outside stringer. Keep the bolt holes at least 2 inches from the edge of the stringer and framing timbers.

At the bottom of the stairs toenail the bottom of the stringers to the subflooring or flooring to provide stability at both ends of the stairs. The stairway is then ready for use, unless you choose to install supports under the stairs. You can do so by cutting timbers with a straight edge for the floor and with an angle cut for the stringers.

Stand the timber in place and mark along the underside of the stringer onto the timber. Cut at that point and you will have a good fit. Use 2-×-6 stock or 4-×-4 stock if available.

Chapter **8**

Framing home additions

A home addition is usually a serious undertaking for any do-it-yourselfer. Such a project represents a huge investment of time, energy, and money, and affects the appearance and utilitarian aspects of the house.

Because the addition will change the external appearance of the house, in many areas city laws require that you have a building permit. Some laws require you to post the permit in a conspicuous place near the building site. Check with the city hall or county courthouse before beginning work.

Your cost for adding a room to an existing house will vary greatly. In some parts of the country a single room addition can easily cost more than $40,000, while in others the cost might be less than $5,000. In both cases the cost of labor is one of the most significant expenses the homeowner will bear. Remember that labor represents at least half the cost when building a house. In too many cases the labor also accounts for a considerable amount of needless damage to the already-expensive building materials. In other words, regard workmanship on a home addition as important as the construction of the entire house. Plan the addition carefully and take whatever steps you can to save money on building materials, as well as energy and frustration on your part.

PLANNING THE ADDITION

Start by determining what the major usage of the addition will be, and consider the implications of every phase of the work. Remember that if you intend to build a family room but want to include a closet for convenience of guests, the building code might well interpret the room with a closet as a potential bedroom. You could then find that your septic tank, if you have one, is no longer adequate, because many codes state that any room with a closet can be considered a bedroom. The reasoning behind the ruling is not totally illogical. While your family might intend to use the room as a den or recreation room, if you ever sell the house the new own-ers may opt to convert the room into a bedroom, particularly if there is a closet in it. The need for another bedroom suggests a large family and excessive demands on the septic tank capacity.

Consider the traffic pattern or flow of the room. Examine the entrances into the room, the location of the windows, the location of the fireplace, if any, and how furniture can be arranged for best service in the room. Examine the methods by which the roof of the new room can be connected to the existing roof. Consider the fire safety exiting plan. Think about the manner in which you will attach the new walls to the existing walls. Consider the elevation of the floor. If the building lot slopes uphill behind the house, you need to determine that the new room will be high enough off the ground to be protected against decay and ter-mite or other insect damage. Look at all the physical implications of the exterior walls of the new room, and then examine the interior implica-tions.

If the room is to be a family room or den, decide where the windows will be placed, how high and how wide they will be, and how they will affect the furniture to be used in the room. Decide, if possible, where doors, light fixtures, and other facets of the room will be located.

Consider the size of the room in terms of materials you plan to use. If you have more than a 16-foot span, you will need supports under ceiling and floor joists, unless you use timbers larger than 2 × 10. You can use 2-×-10 lumber for spans up to 16 feet. If you decide that the room will be 18 feet wide, you will then have to install a girder and use shorter joists. If you decide to make the room 15 feet wide, you will not need a girder but you will need to cut off a foot from each joist. You will be wasting the extra foot unless you have a later use for the scrap lumber.

Remember to plan the room with length and width divisible by four. This means that unless the length and width are 12, 16, 20, or other num-ber divisible by four, you will have to cut many pieces of timber or wall covering in order to make them fit. You will not only waste materials, but your time and energy as well.

If the room is 15 feet wide, you will need to cut off 1 foot from the paneling or other wall covering and you will have no real use for the odd foot of paneling stock. The same will hold true for Sheetrock and every other wall covering that comes in 4-foot widths, and applies to ceilings and floors as well as walls.

Think about window and door openings while you are planning. If you use a 36-inch door with a 40-inch rough door opening, you might find that you will need to trim or cut paneling in order to get a proper fit. You could relocate the door or modify the length of the wall, if doing so will not affect the rest of the planning adversely, so that you will have a good fit for all wall covering materials.

Use the same planning for windows. While windows sometimes should be located at a particular spot for aesthetic reasons, the location can produce difficulties in wall construction that might be solved if the window was moved a few inches to the left or right.

If you plan to use concrete or cement blocks for walls, plan so that you can use a full length of blocks in every other course. Try not to have a wall length that will cause you to have to cut or break a block in each course. Breaking blocks takes time. It can also be very frustrating because blocks are easily ruined if broken incorrectly.

If possible and feasible, consider floor lengths in terms of tiles or other floor coverings you plan to use. If you can avoid cutting tiles, you also cut your work and worry considerably. The same is true of ceiling tiles that will have to be cut when you are ready to install ceilings.

You can either cost yourself or save yourself money by planning the room carefully in terms of joists. Each joist will cost you $10 or more, plus delivery fee in some instances. If you have to space joists oddly, you will also encounter difficulties when it is time to install insulation.

Consider how the room might be used in the future. Perhaps your family size is such that you do not need an added bedroom, but in a few years the added room might be a necessity. Think about adding a room that can be converted into a bedroom or any other type of room when the need arises.

You can make some allowances for future needs by installing a bathroom or half bath as part of your planning for the addition. If you do not want to complete the bathroom, do the rough plumbing work and add the rest later, if needed.

Also consider how the addition of the room will affect the future sale of the house, in case you decide to relocate. The addition will appeal to a larger family.

What activities will occur in the room? If the room is to be used primarily for a television entertainment area, you can plan to add cabinets to hold the television set. What about a billiard table, stereo components, computer equipment, or the need for a gathering place for the family on special occasions?

You should give some thought to the heating system, the duct areas, water lines—if any—electrical wiring, appliances and their locations, large furniture pieces, and any other elements of the room you will need to work around. Careful planning can make the added room a source of anticipation and pleasure rather than one of frustration.

LAYING OFF THE ADDITION

You frame an addition to your house as you framed the house when you constructed it, with one major difference: You must devise a method of joining the addition to the house without creating a visual discrepancy that is displeasing.

Measuring and squaring the corners

Start by staking off the room area carefully, remembering to have room dimensions divisible by four. Run one line parallel to the existing house and to a point 3 feet past where the addition ends—if the new room is to be an extension of one of the existing house walls. Move to the opposite wall that will be parallel to the one laid off and run another line, again 3 feet past the end of the wall line. Check at both of the existing corners where the new room will join the existing house to be sure that the corners are square. You can use a transit if you have one. If not, measure carefully diagonally across the corners.

The easiest way is to measure from one corner to a point 7 feet down the line. Do the same on the line represented by the existing house wall. Then measure diagonally across the corner from each point. The distance should be 10 feet (FIG. 8-1).

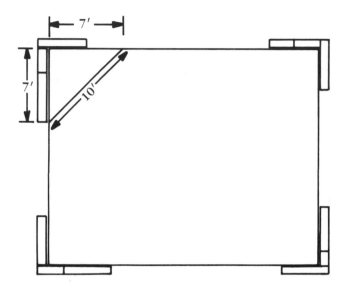

8-1 A simple way to determine whether a corner is square.

There are a few ways to check the distances. Use a piece of cardboard or a sheet of paper. Take a 1-foot ruler and measure to a point along one side of the page. Then measure down the other side. Mark the points and then measure across diagonally from point to point. All you need to do then is translate inches into feet. Remember that the distance diagonally should not be longer than your ruler. By using this method, you can devise your own formula for squaring any corner.

When both corners are squared, run a line from the two lines laid off already. Run the line 3 feet past the point where the lines intersect. Be sure these corners are square (FIG. 8-2).

Double-check for squareness by measuring diagonally from one corner across the room to the far corner. Write down the exact measurement, even to fractional inches. Then measure diagonally in the opposite direction and write down the results, again to the closest fractional inch. Compare the distances. They should be exactly the same.

Use a plumb marker to mark the exact point where the corner lines cross. You can make a plumb marker or plumb bob by sticking a pin into the eraser of a pencil and then attaching a string to the pin. Hold the string

8-2 Construct batter boards then stretch nylon twine tightly from corner to corner in order to check for squareness.

at the exact point where the lines cross and lower the pencil slowly and steadily until the point touches the ground. This point is your first corner point. Do the same at the other corner or corners. When you are finished you can drive a stake about a foot long into the ground at each of the marked corner points. Run a strong line to each stake to mark the outline of the room.

Marking the footings

Follow the line, using a can to drop marking powder to mark the footing lines. You can use lime, fertilizer, flour, sand, or any other material that can be seen clearly. When all lines are marked, you can take down the stakes and begin digging the footings. Proceed as you would if you were framing a new house.

There is one matter of concern at this point. You must either set the piers or foundation wall so that it will be the exact height of the foundation walls of the existing house, or you must arrange to install a step leading from one room to another. If the house is built on a severe slope, you might find that you will encounter considerable difficulties. If the land slopes upward behind the house, you might have to dig very deep footings and also build the addition close to the ground. If the land slopes in the opposite direction, you might have a very high foundation wall at the far end of the addition.

Establishing a level foundation line

After the footings are dug and poured, decide on a foundation wall plan. The first step is to establish a level line from the existing foundation wall to the end of the one being readied. If the two wall lines are not level, you will encounter severe problems as you proceed with the block laying.

One easy way to arrive at a level line is to drive a stake into the ground a foot or so beyond the end of the footings and in line with the foundation wall of the existing house. Be sure that the top of the stake is at least as high as the existing foundation wall.

Drive a mortar or masonry nail between the foundation wall and the sill of the house. If you cannot get to the point, drive the nail into the mortar of the first course. Attach a string to the nail and run the string to the stake. Fasten it only temporarily so you can move the string up and down on the stake as necessary.

Between the stake and the foundation wall drive two more stakes, one at the one-third point and the other at the two-thirds point. Lay a perfectly straight 2 × 4 so that one end is resting on top of the nail in the mortar joint. Hold the other end steadily and place a level on top of it (FIG. 8-3). With the end of the timber pressed against the first stake, move the end up and down until you have a level reading. Use a pencil to mark the bottom of the timber and drive a nail to mark the point. Move the timber so that the bottom rests on the nail in the stake and the other end is pressed against the second stake. Again, find the level mark and mark the point with a nail, as you did before. Do this again until you reach the end of the room line.

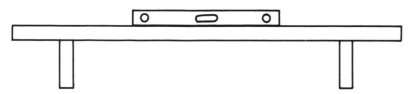

8-3   For a wide expanse that requires an accurate level reading, use a straight timber across the footings stakes to be sure that all stake tops are level.

This is a difficult way to achieve a level line, but it works if you do not have access to a transit and someone to help you. Remember that you have marked the level of the bottom of the first block, not the top. When you are laying blocks you should bear in mind that you still have to lay an additional course after you reach the level line in order for the foundation wall to be level with the foundation wall of the house.

You can follow this method around the entire wall. Drive stakes along the second wall line and again use the straight edge and the level to get the exact reading.

When you are ready to mark the third wall line, start at the foundation wall of the house and use the nail again in the mortar joint. Drive the stakes and set the line as you did earlier. When you reach the end of the wall line, as you reach the corner where the second wall line was marked, your level line should meet the other line at exactly the same place. If the two lines do not meet properly, you have erred in your marking or the foundation wall of the house is not level.

If necessary, mark your fourth line (the one along the foundation wall of the existing house) as you did the other three. You can quickly determine if the error was yours or the mason's who did the foundation walls.

Laying foundation walls

You are now ready to lay the foundation walls. Mark the board or 2 × 4 where each course should reach and begin work. Use a block line to keep your work aligned perfectly. Remember that each block should come as close as possible to the string without actually touching it. The top of the block should also be perfectly level with the block line.

When you planned the room, one of the considerations was that you need a wall line that will permit you to lay whole blocks or halves. When the footings are ready, tentatively lay blocks along the footings to see that you can lay whole blocks in the first course, all around the wall lines.

If the first wall is 15 feet long, you will have 180 inches. A block and its mortar joint will take up 16 inches. You will have room for 11 whole blocks and one 1/4 block. Such a block is difficult to cut or break. If possible, lengthen the room to 16 feet, which will be 192 inches. You can lay 12 whole blocks and not have to break one. You will also have a much easier and more economical time when you start to install wall covering, tiles, and other materials that come in 4-foot widths.

Lay the blocks of the second course so that at the corners the final block will lap over the block below it by one-half the block length. This is necessary for bonding purposes. You might find that you have to break a block in half, which is not too difficult. You can buy blocks with an extra partition in them so that you can break them easily. You can also order block halves, so when you place your order ask the dealer to include halves for your convenience.

Remember to hold the joints and bonds as you work. This means that you should keep your joints the same thickness, when possible, and that the bonding should be the same at every point. The mortar joint in the course you are laying should come in the exact center of the block below, and it should align exactly with the mortar joint two courses below. This pattern will hold true all along the wall (FIG. 8-4).

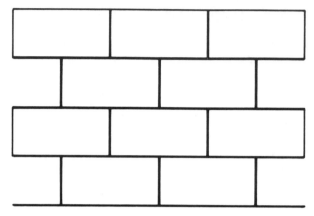

8-4 These are proper bonding joints. Never allow ends or blocks to be even with each other.

Remember to check the level of blocks from front to back and from side to side. Use your level to be sure that the wall is perfectly vertical. When you are laying blocks it is very easy to allow one block corner to remain high or one end to slide over slightly as the mortar shifts under pressure. Pay constant attention to the alignment of the wall.

Remember to joint your work before the mortar has a chance to dry. This means that if you are working on a very hot day you should stop and joint every hour or so. If you do not have a jointer, you can use a brick or a short length of 2 × 4. Hold the brick or 2-x-4 section so that one corner can be inserted into the masonry joint. Rub the brick or block in the joints until you have a neat, clean joint. Rub both vertical and horizontal joints.

At the end of the work day, or twice a day if the weather is hot, place a brick flat against the wall and rub it vigorously back and forth across the wall to dislodge any mortar particles that have stuck to the wall. These particles can be cleaned easily at this point but are much harder to dislodge later. After rubbing the wall surface with a brick, use a brush with stiff bristles to clean away any clinging dust or tiny particles. This final step will leave the wall clean and neat.

Be particularly careful with the final course in the foundation wall. When you are laying lower courses and you have a mortar joint slightly thin or thick, you can adjust by changing the joints in the next course. At the top course no adjustments can be made in such a fashion.

Use your level, story pole, and guide lines regularly to be sure that your top work is level and plumb. When this is done, you can start to install the joists and sills.

INSTALLING SILLS AND JOISTS

For this part of the work use treated lumber that is decay resistant and resistant to moisture and similar problems. Wood that is in constant contact with concrete seems to decay quickly, but the treated lumber will not be subject to such problems. The cost is slightly greater, but the durability of the wood makes it a bargain at the increased price.

Sills

Use 2-×-8 timbers that will cover the blocks completely. If you want double insurance against wind damage, install anchor bolts. The traditional anchor bolt will be firmly entrenched in mortar or concrete to a depth of 8 inches or slightly less. Most builders feel that this is adequate protection.

One easy way to install anchor bolts is to fill a block with mortar or concrete and then set the installed bolt into place. Here's how to handle this operation: Lay a sill timber on top of the foundation wall and slide it over so that the holes in the blocks are clearly visible. Decide which block you will install the anchor bolts in and use a carpenter's pencil to mark the location on the top edge of the block and also on the sill.

Many builders recommend using an anchor bolt every 2 feet, while others feel that every 3 or 4 feet is sufficient. When the sill and block are both marked, fill the block hole with concrete or mortar. You might need to wedge a flat section of a block into the hole in order to keep the mortar from falling all the way to the bottom of the wall.

Fill all blocks where bolts will be installed. Then use a chalk line down the center of the sill to mark the middle of the timber. Where you marked the sill on the edge, also make another mark on the chalk line.

Drill a hole all the way through the sill. Use a bit that is only slightly larger than the bolts you are using. You can now countersink the bolts or allow the nuts to remain above the surface of the sill. To countersink them, use a bit that is larger than the washers you will use on the bolts and drill a hole that is equal to the thickness of the nut and washer. Usually slightly more than 1/4 inch will be sufficient (FIG. 8-5).

Push the threaded end of the bolt up through the hole and insert the washer, then add the nut. Tighten the nut until the end of the bolt is even with the top of the nut. Do this with all bolts, and when the sill is ready, you can set it in place and the bolts will sink into the still-wet mortar or concrete. If the bolts do not sink readily, tap the nut with a hammer until it is seated fully.

If you want to have greater protection, buy some threaded rods. These usually cost 50 cents per foot, so each rod will cost you a dollar because you need a 2-foot section for each bolt location. Buy washers that will fit the rods and also washers that are much larger than the rod. Buy the largest you can find as long as the first washer will not slip through the hole of the second washer.

When the sill holes are drilled, put a large washer over the end of the threaded rod and add the regular washer. Add the nut to hold both wash-

8-5 Drill attachments are available that will drill the basic hole for the bolt and then drill a larger hole to countersink the nut.

ers in place. Push the threaded rod end down into the hole in the blocks until only 2 inches are left above the top of the final block. Hold the rod in place while you use a trowel to shovel mortar into the hole until it is filled to the top.

Place the sill carefully over the rods. Guide the sill into place so that the rods push up through the holes in the sill. Seat the sill and add a washer and nut. When the mortar has hardened, you can tighten the nuts to draw the sill firmly into position (FIG. 8-6).

You now have the equivalent of not one but six blocks holding the bolts in place. A wind would have to be strong enough to pull the bolts

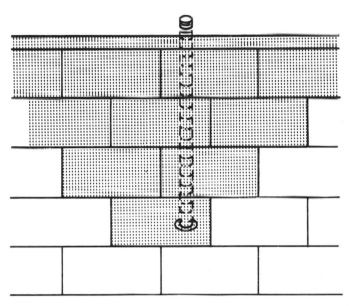

8-6 The shaded blocks represent those that are tied together by the threaded bolt. The bolt should have a large washer and nut on the bottom end to provide resistance to the mortar or concrete.

and washers through several inches of mortar or concrete and also break the bond of three courses of blocks.

If you do not want to use threaded rods at every point, use three or four of them in each wall and regular anchor bolts for the rest of the wall. You will still have adequate protection.

Joists

When the sills are in place, you are ready to install the headers and joists. The headers are essentially joists standing on the sills. They form the outer perimeter of the room. The purpose of the header is to prevent an open space between sill and subflooring and to hold the outer boundary of the house securely in place.

Stand the first header timber on edge and toenail it to the sill. It should be flush with the outer edge of the sill and as plumb or vertical as you can get it. Minor adjustments can be made later. Stand the first header timber at the corner of the wall and stand the next one so that it abuts the end of the first one. Nail the two together by driving nails through the end of one timber and into the other one. You can also toenail the second timber to the sill.

Install the rest of the header timbers and then lay off the joist locations. Remember that joists should be spaced so that they are 16 inches on center. Decide which direction you need to run the joists, then mark locations.

If your room is 16 feet wide, remember that you will have 192 inches of floor space from one outside wall to the other. If you divide 16 into 192 you will get 12. You already have the joist or header timbers in place, so you will need only 11 joists.

Install the 11 joists as you did earlier. Mark both header timbers, then make certain that the ends of the joists fall at the exact markings. Be particularly careful with any joists that fall at the 48, 96, and all other 48-inch gradations. These are the joists where the subflooring panels will be nailed, and you need to have them spaced exactly.

Remember that you are measuring from the outside edge of the headers or joists that form the perimeter of the house. When you have laid off the first joist markings, double-check to see that the center of the third new joist (the fourth, counting the header) is at the 48-inch mark. If it is not, make the necessary adjustments at this point.

When you have completed nailing in the joists, you are ready to install subflooring.

INSTALLING SUBFLOORING

Whether you are working on a room addition or a full house, the subflooring principles remain the same. Position the first panel (if you are using plywood subflooring) so that the edges of the panel are flush with the outside edges of the header timbers. Also, the inner long edge of the panel should run down the center of the joist at the 48-inch mark.

Some builders suggest that you install the subflooring by nailing only the four corners down. The argument is that if the subflooring gets rained on several times, it will buck and separate if it is nailed fully. Others contend that the more securely the subflooring is nailed, the less likely it is to buck. The recommendation here is to nail the panels fully, using a nail every foot or so along all joists.

One helpful tip is to use the chalk line to mark the plywood along the joist path. Attach one end of the chalk line to the center of the joist and hold the other end at the center of the point where the joist was nailed to the header. You can then drive nails through the chalk line and never have to worry about missing the joist.

Make the chalk line at every joist that cannot be seen. By doing so you are assured that your nails will hit the joist for a firm hold and that you are not punching needless holes in the plywood and wasting nails and time.

If you planned your room well, you will have space for full panels of plywood to fit perfectly onto the joists and headers. You should not have to cut any of the panels or use any partial panels in order to cover the joists fully. It is usually recommended that you leave small cracks about the thickness of a quarter between the panels to allow for swelling if the subflooring is dampened.

FINISHING UP

When subflooring is down, you can proceed to frame the walls as you did for the first part of the house. If you have never framed a house or even a room, lay off the framing for the studding and sole plates as you did for the joists.

Lay two long 2-×-4 timbers side by side along the length of a wall. Mark a space at the end of each for the corner posts (the equivalent of two 2-×-4 timbers), and mark a 16-inch center for the remainder of the studs in the wall. Mark both of the 2-×-4 timbers because one will become the sole plate and the other will be the top plate.

Double-check your work. The stud locations should correspond exactly with those of the joists so that every stud you install should be located precisely above the joist.

When the sole plate and top plate are marked, separate them so that you can lay a 2-×-4 stud between them. When you are ready to nail in the studs, position the end of each stud so that it is in the spot previously marked for it. Drive nails through the bottom of the sole plate and through the top of the top plate and into the ends of the studs. In this fashion install all studs and corner posts. See Chapter 3 for additional details.

When all studs and corner posts are in position, you are ready to raise the wall assembly and nail the sole plate to the subflooring. With the assembly standing and adequately braced or securely held, use a large hammer to tap the sole plate until the outer edge of it is in perfect alignment with the edge of the subflooring. Nail the sole plate to the subflooring and install temporary braces to hold the framed assembly in place until the rest of the wall can be framed.

Consult Chapter 3 for details on how to assemble and install all cripple studs, top caps, and bracing or bridging. Install all rough window and door openings.

You are now ready to install the ceiling joists. When you nail in the top caps, leave room for any partition walls you plan to include in the structure. Because you are at this point framing only one room, you probably will not have a partition wall.

The final work in this area is to install the ceiling joists. These are to be nailed in place directly above the studs and spaced 16 inches on center, just as the studs and floor joists were. Proper spacing makes it much easier for you to lay in the insulation later. If you do not space properly, you will find that you either have to cut the insulation to make it fit or leave cracks that will allow heating and cooling to escape.

If you install hanging joists, remember never to notch the joist more than one-third of its width. You will probably need to mark the joist locations as you did before to ensure proper spacing. Nail in the joists and use any bridging you wish to stabilize the timbers.

You are now ready to leave the framing work on the walls and concentrate on framing any special aspects of the room, such as closets.

Chapter **9**

Framing closets

Of all the areas in a house, closets certainly rank among the most useful and also among the least planned. Before you start to frame a closet, ask yourself the obvious questions: What will the closet be used for? Who will use it and how frequently? How adaptable is the closet to change? If you are willing to do some serious planning, you can make use of virtually every vacant space in your house by adding closets, cabinets, and shelves.

Every bedroom obviously needs a closet, just as every kitchen and every bathroom need cabinets. There are many other areas in the house that need closets or other storage space, and you can construct this space with a minimum of expense.

Start planning with the bedroom closets. Determine the size of these closets according to who will be using them. If a teenager will be using the closet, chances are that considerably more space will be needed than if an elderly person uses the closet. A walk-in closet is far more serviceable to a person whose wardrobe is very extensive than it would be to a person who seldom dresses for social occasions.

Consider how much space in the room can be spared for the closet. If the bedroom is 12-×-12 feet and you need to build a closet 3 feet deep along the entire wall, you will leave virtually no room for anything but the most basic furnishings in the bedroom. Solve the problem by building a small closet that extends into the room, then use the leftover wall space for a chest of drawers or other furniture that can be placed out of the traffic pattern.

A BASIC BEDROOM CLOSET

The easiest way to frame a bedroom closet is by using a back-to-back arrangement so that two adjoining bedrooms can use the same wall for a closet, and each bedroom can claim one-half of the closet area. If your house is 32 feet wide, it is likely that the space on one end of the house will be devoted to two bedrooms, a hallway, and the closets that serve both bedrooms. There is also a chance that the bathrooms will be back-to-back on a wall that is common to both bedrooms.

Many people have built homes under the theory that the bedroom is the one room where family members spend the least amount of waking time. They feel that because the bedroom is used in a very practical sense the least amount of time, it should be as small as possible and still be serviceable. Such a viewpoint can be challenged from several directions. A basement is used under usual conditions very little; days may pass without having family members actually enter the basement, but this lack of constant use does not in any way diminish the value of the basement. A formal dining room is very seldom used, but such a room is often one of the focal spots in the entire house. A formal living room is often reserved for only special guests and in many homes it is not used for weeks at a time. The bedroom, however, is generally used every day, and the larger the bedroom, the greater the chance that it will be used more. If the room is large enough, it can contain an entertainment center featuring a television set, stereo equipment, bookshelves, and even a work desk.

Determining size and design

Before you choose to make your bedroom small, consider what uses might be made of the area before you complete the framing. Many people feel that a 16-×-16 foot bedroom is far too large to be practical. However, keep in mind that with this size you could have an 8-foot closet on one wall. The room that adjoins it can also have a similarly large closet.

To frame such a pair of closets, decide which room will lose the space required for the closet and then determine how deep the closet should be. If you decide that the closet should be 30 inches deep, start at the wall framing and measure 30 inches into the room from both corners. Mark the spot.

Determine whether the closets will have traditional doors, folding doors, or sliding doors. Use a chalk line to mark across the floor from the point where the closet extends into the room 30 inches. If the wall is 16 feet long and you want two 8-foot closets, find two 16-foot, 2-×-4 timbers and lay them side by side on the subflooring. Mark the points where the studs will be located as you did with the wall framing. Mark both 2 × 4s.

Separate the 2 × 4s so that you can place studs between them at the desired points. Do not forget to frame in the rough door opening for both closets. Use regular 16-inch on-center spacing for studs.

Installation

Install the studs and then nail in the rough door opening. Include the cripple stud, if any, or the header above the doorway. While the assembled door is still lying on the floor, cut four 26-inch lengths of 2 × 4. Nail two of these to the floor, one against each corner and extending into the room. Your closet will be slightly less than 30 inches deep because the actual size of the framing timbers is the milled rather than the nominal size (FIG. 9-1).

When the two pieces are installed, raise the wall assembly and tap the bottom 2 × 4 (the sole plate) until it is firmly positioned against the two

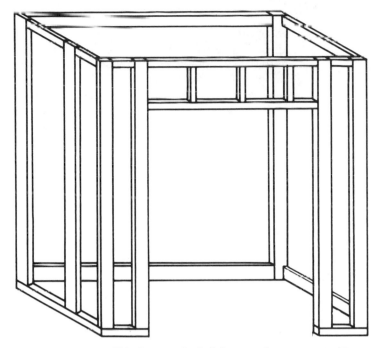

9-1   A simple closet design. This closet can be built into a wall or constructed in a corner of a room.

pieces of 2 × 4 you nailed in. Nail the sole plate to the subflooring and also toenail the sole plate to the shorter lengths installed against the floor.

You can now install the other two short lengths of 2 × 4 at the top of the wall frame just as you nailed them to the floor. This time nail them to the framing at the ceiling instead of the floor. If you plan to use sliding doors, you will not need to install studs along the entire front of the framing. Instead of studs, use an extra-long header over the doorway.

If the other half of the closet is to open into the adjoining room, remove the studs to allow for the doorway. Be sure to install a header over the doorway leading to the second half of the closet.

If you want to frame a smaller closet in one corner of the room, frame it just as you would a small room. Use the same plan of sole plate, top plate, studs, cripple studs, and header over the doorway. The second half of the wall space (the part not used by the closet) can then be used for a dresser or chest of drawers, or for a desk or similar item of furniture.

CABINETS

In bathrooms or other areas where cabinet space on the floor is a necessity, you can frame these in much the same way as closets were framed. Determine the depth and length of the cabinet, then mark the dimensions on the floor using a chalk line or straightedge and pencil.

Construction

Assume that the depth of the cabinet is 28 inches, the length 60 inches, and the height 30 inches. Frame the front of the cabinet as if you were framing a wall. Start with the sole plate and top plate as well as the corner posts. Use one single length of 2 × 4 for corners. Lay the two 60-inch timbers on the floor and then cut five sections of 28-inch 2 × 4s. Position these short ''studs'' as if you were framing a wall and nail them together (FIG. 9-2).

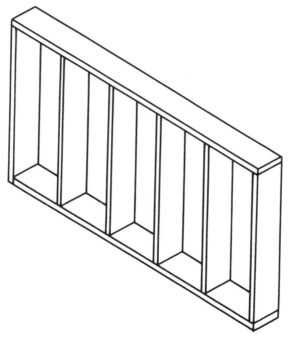

9-2   Cabinet framing is very much like framing a small room. The basic ''wall'' of the cabinet is composed of materials similar to headers and studs.

Set the framing aside and construct another assembly just like the first one. This one is to be used at the back of the cabinet and against the wall.

The depth of the cabinet is 28 inches, so you will need to cut four lengths of 2 × 4 24 inches long. Your actual depth will be slightly less than 28 inches because the 2 × 4 used for the sole plate and top plate sections is actually less than 4 inches wide.

These 24-inch lengths are to be used as sole plate and top plate for the sides of the cabinet. Nail the back frame assembly to the wall by positioning the framing so that one corner post is in the corner of the room. Drive nails through the corner post and into the stud behind the wall covering. Fasten the sole plate to the floor by driving nails down through the 2 × 4s and into the subflooring or flooring. Locate studs behind the cabinet framing and drive nails through the framing timbers and into the studding.

The back frame is now in position. Next, locate the front framing so that the corner post is against the wall and 24 inches from the corner. To be sure of the exact location, lay one of the 24-inch lengths of 2 × 4 against the wall so that it abuts the back framing. The front framing should now back into the 2 × 4 you just put in place.

Nail the sole plate of the front framing on the subflooring or flooring so that the framing will stand alone. Nail the short 2-×-4 lengths to the floor, then toenail the front framing to the side 2 × 4 you just installed.

On the other end of the cabinet do the same thing. When this is finished, nail in the top lengths of 2 × 4 so the 24-inch sections are fastened securely to the back framing and to the front framing. You can now also nail in stud sections to divide the side framing of the cabinet.

These steps for building a floor cabinet have been stated in terms of framing a room, in order to make them more familiar and easier to convey. Cabinets like closets, can be thought of as miniature rooms. Continue the comparison by nailing in short lengths of 2 × 4s (24 inches long) between the front and back framing as if the new pieces were ceiling joists. They should be positioned between the top plates of the framing and installed no more than 16 inches apart on center.

The framing is now complete. When you are ready, nail plywood or other wall coverings over the framing. In the front you can install doors that open and close over the 16-inch on-center framing. The doors will be about 14 1/2 inches wide and about 26 inches tall. You can have as many as four doors and they can vary in width (FIG. 9-3).

Such a cabinet is framed very strongly and will withstand a great deal of pressure. It will be strong enough to serve as a table surface for storage,

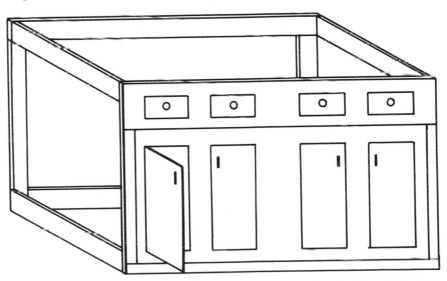

9-3 The cabinet doors open and close over the 16-inch center framing. The widths of the doors can be varied.

and you can put shelves inside. To shelve the framing, use 2-×-4 stock for maximum strength. Plywood makes a good top for such a cabinet.

CLOSETS UNDER STAIRWAYS

Where your stairs are located, there is generally a large amount of wasted space underneath the stringers. With a little effort this space can be converted into neat and useful closets or cabinets. The cabinet framing can, at the same time, strengthen the stairway against excessive weight damage. The space is flexible enough that you can use any part of it or all of it for closet or cabinet space. You can have a combination of closets and cabinets.

The location of the stairway will have some influence on how you use the space beneath it. If the stairway is in a formal part of the house, you can convert the space to a cloak closet or a glass-doored cabinet for special china or vases. If the stairs are in the basement, the space can be used for tool storage, as a small pantry, or as a cabinet for odds and ends that have no place upstairs (FIG. 9-4).

To frame in the entire space as a closet, first locate several 2 × 4s ranging in length from 2 feet up to 8 or 9 feet. You will need two of each length cut for the early part of the framing.

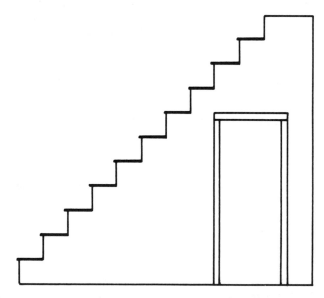

9-4 A closet can be constructed under a stairway. The higher part of the closet can be used for coats and the lower part for boots, tools, or other small items.

Installation

Again, compare the framing process to that of framing a room. The cabinets and closets presented here are strong, durable, and useful; they are not the highly ornate and decorative cabinets used to hold delicate materials.

The first step is to nail in the "sole plates" as if you were framing a room. Use a straightedge to mark a plate line from the lowest point of the stringers to the wall under the highest point in the stairway. Cut two of these timbers. If you want a perfect fit, lay the 2 × 4s so that they extend slightly past the lowest point of the stringers. Reach under the stringers and mark the stringer slant by using the bottom edge of the stringer as a guide so that you can mark the 2-×-4 length.

Cut along the slanted line and the 2 × 4 should slip neatly into the angle formed by the floor and stringer. When you have cut 2 × 4s for both sides of the closet or cabinet, nail these in place by driving nails through the 2-×-4 plates and into the flooring. You are now ready to measure, mark, cut, and install the basic framing for the cabinet area.

Start by sawing a squared end on two 2 × 4s that are long enough to reach from the plate to the bottom of the stairway stringers against the wall or at the highest point. Stand one 2 × 4 so that the squared end is resting squarely on the plate. The top end is against the wall and should extend slightly beyond the bottom of the stringer. Reach behind the 2 × 4 and mark the slanting cut line by using the stringer edge as your guide. Take the 2 × 4 down and set it aside. Use another 2 × 4 on the other stringer and mark it the same way. Cut both 2 × 4s along the slanted line and nail these in place by fitting them under the stringers and upon the plate. Fasten the upright 2 × 4s by nailing through them and into the wall.

Measure and cut other 2 × 4s to fit every 16 inches on-center from the wall to the angle formed by the floor and stringer. Install these "studs" as if you were framing a room. When framing is completed, you can cover the walls with paneling, plywood, or whatever other wall coverings you prefer.

You should frame a rough door opening in the room side of the stairway. First determine what size door you want, then double-stud the opening on each side. You can install a header for more strength above the door.

You can, if you prefer, frame a closet from the taller section and a cabinet from the lower sections. To frame a closet, cut and install the plate timbers, then install the upright 2 × 4s that serve as studs. Mark the plate for 16-inch on-center locations and frame in the rough door opening. Many doors are 36 inches wide and require a 40-inch rough opening, but you might be able to use a smaller door for the closet.

Determine the door size needed and allow 4 inches of rough opening in addition to the width of the door. Allow an extra 2 inches of height for the door and install a header. See earlier details on header construction.

Continue framing as far as you wish the closet to run. If the closet is to be 5 feet long, at the 5-foot point on the plate mark the point and stand a 2 × 4 so that it is perfectly vertical and also rests against the stringer. Then mark the 2 × 4 using the lower edge of the stringer as a guide.

Cut and install two studs at this point, then measure the distance between the two plates and cut two 2-×-4 lengths to fit inside the plates. Cut the lengths and install them so that the inside edge is even with the inside edge of the studding just installed. Install one of the shorter 2 × 4s on the floor and between the plates and another at the top of the studding and between the studding so that the 2 × 4 is located just below the stringer lower edge.

Cut and install any studding that you would like to install for that end of the closet and add any joist work you wish for the ceiling of the closet. When the closet is completely studded and the rough door opening is framed, you are ready either to install the wall covering or to frame the adjacent cabinet.

You will probably have a considerable amount of storage space above the door of the closet. An ideal way to utilize that space is to install the basic framing as you did for the present closet and then add door framing for a very small access door. The door can be a standard rectangle, or you can even shape it to conform to the triangular shape of the opening. Plan for the latch to be placed on the narrow side of the door and the hinges to be located near the wall or on the higher side of the stairway.

You can allow the area above the door to remain one large storage space, or you can add shelf framing. To do so, simply install 2 × 4s parallel to the floor on both sides of the opening and lay shelves on the 2 × 4s.

In the area to the side of the closet you have enough space for a triangular-shaped cabinet. After you have installed the plates and the studding, frame a rough door opening. You might want to install double doors and leave the stud in the center for a closing base for the doors. The area inside the cabinet can be shelved or left as one large opening, depending upon what is to be stored there.

A HALLWAY CLOSET

If you have space at the end of a hallway, you can frame in the space as if you were adding a tiny room. Measure the distance across the hallway and mark and cut a plate timber to be installed there. Do the same with a cap timber. After the plate 2 × 4 is installed you can cut the studding for the wall area. Stand a 2 × 4 on the plate and extend it up the wall in a plumb fashion and nail it to the wall framing. Do this on both sides of the hallway.

Across the top of the upright 2 × 4s nail the plate timber. Then add any rough door framing that is necessary. Install a header above the door as space permits. Add double studding on both sides of the doors.

For shelving ease, use short lengths of 2 × 4 fastened upright on each side of the closet. Then install a 2 × 4 parallel to the floor so that it rests upon the top edges of the upright 2 × 4s. You can later lay shelves on the 2 × 4s on each side of the closet.

If you have the available stock, cut lengths of 1-×-10 boards and lay them on edge so that they fit into the closet neatly, then lay other boards across the edges for shelving.

OTHER POSSIBILITIES

Throughout the house and carport or garage there are recesses or alcoves that serve little if any functional purpose. Any of these areas can be framed for closet or cabinet space easily and can be used to store linens, lingerie, books, important papers, or any of the other dozens of items around the house that should be protected.

If there is a large recess in a wall and you feel that it could serve better as a closet or cabinet, all you need to do is cut and install the plates and caps, add the studding, and frame in the rough door opening and double-stud it. Such work requires only a few minutes of time and virtually no expertise beyond the ability to use a hammer and saw.

The back of a garage or carport is often an ideal place for a storage room or large closet or cabinet. Frame the opening as you would a room in the house. When you are ready, install outdoor or exterior wall covering. Use an exterior door and insulate the storage area as if you were weatherproofing a room in the house. You might decide later to house the washing machine in the area and you do not want the pipes to freeze. If the space is to be used to store canned fruit and vegetables, you want to keep the room warm enough that the fluids in the jars will not freeze and break the containers.

If you need a large work surface for desk work in a room, you can frame a long cabinet across the end of a room and leave one sector open for knee room. The remainder of the cabinet can be used for ordinary storage. You can do the same with a workshop work surface. Here you will also need to leave knee room if you intend to sit while you work. The cabinet space can be used for storing tools, nuts and bolts, and the other gear used in the workshop.

USING SCRAP MATERIALS

As you work at framing your house, you undoubtedly collect numerous short or small pieces of boards, timbers, paneling, Sheetrock, tile, and other leftover materials. Save all scraps until you are completely finished with the house. You will find that many apparently useless bits of lumber can be used in closet or basic cabinet work. Between shelves you often need lengths of 2 × 4s or boards that are no longer than 6 to 10 inches. You can use foot-long lengths of studding materials for cripple studs over doors or under windows.

Small sections of plywood can be used as wall covers for smaller closets or cabinets. If the closet is small there will often be a need for a strip of paneling 12 to 15 inches wide to be installed on each side of a door. If you can use a scrap piece of lumber and keep from cutting a 2 × 4 or 2 × 6, you have saved a dollar or possibly much more. If you can make use of sections of Sheetrock, you won't have to cut an entire panel.

As you work, store scrap lumber instead of throwing it carelessly to one side. Stack any extra cement blocks so that you have two rows of them, then lay a piece of exterior plywood or leftover tile over the blocks to form a crude storage bin. Put all potentially useful scraps in this bin, then later when you need a small piece of timber you can find it here and you won't have to cut a whole timber.

Chapter **10**

Framing carports and garages

As is true in the cases of basements and porches, many builders feel that building a carport or garage is an exercise in false economy. They point out that the automobile that is protected by the carport during the night must sit in a parking lot all day while the driver is at work, and that the greatest likelihood of damage is from sun rays and similar weather problems that are greater during the day than at night. Another argument against carports and garages is that they are so often used for lawn mowers and numerous other items used in outdoor living—everything except the car.

The major argument in favor of carports and garages is that if you pay $25,000 for an automobile, you want to protect it as much as you can. The car often represents the second greatest investment the owner makes, a house being the first.

The main difference between a garage and carport is that a garage is enclosed so that it can be locked. Often there is also an apartment or storage area above a garage. When you have decided to build a carport or garage, you will quickly notice the basic similarities between framing a room or house and framing a carport. One difference is that the carport often has no walls: it consists of a roof and support posts and little else. The information here will include the complete framing of a carport or garage, leaving the possibility open for enclosing the building or converting it into a spare room.

The best argument for building the garage attached to the house is that if you ever need a family room or extra bedroom, the garage or the porch are convenient for this purpose. The porch is often used because it is already roofed and floored. All that must be done is to install a ceiling and wall covering. The garage is usually selected because it is roofed and has a three wall enclosure already. The garage frequently also has a concrete floor, which will help reduce the time and labor involved in the conversion process.

The carport is usually the last choice for conversion because it often consists of little more than a sloped roof and posts, none of which can be effectively used in a room addition. Therefore the carport we describe here differs from the usual type in that it is more functional.

A BASIC CAR SHELTER

Start with careful planning and measurements. Years ago the carport tended to be fairly small because, while cars were very large and cumbersome, the typical family owned only one car. In recent years the size of cars has diminished but the trend is toward two- and three-car families. When you are planning the carport, consider not only what you have but what the future is likely to bring in terms of automobile ownership. You might be the only driver in the house at the present time, but your spouse may need his or her own car and children growing into adulthood will almost invariably want or need a car. Unless you are virtually positive that you will never need an expansion, start by planning a two-car garage or carport. If possible, also plan to build the shelter very near the house or attached to the house.

Determining size and design

If you choose to build a freestanding car shelter, plan the structure slightly if not significantly larger than you think at first. Allow for the future purchase of a larger car or, for example, a boat and trailer. For a two-car carport, you will need at least 12 feet for each bay. While a typical car is less than 6 feet wide, you must allow for doors on both sides to open and for people to be able to get in and out of the car. A two-car carport would therefore need to be at least 24 feet wide.

There should be sufficient length to allow the car to be pulled fully into the shelter with room to spare. The typical mid-size car is about 15 feet long, and many full-size cars and trucks are 18 feet long. The shelter should then be 20 to 24 feet long. If you are contemplating the purchase of a boat, the shelter should be even longer, depending upon the size of the boat.

Also remember that dimensions should be divisible by four. If you choose to build a shelter 22 feet long, in most instances you will purchase the materials for a 24-foot shelter. The only real extra costs between 22 and 24 feet will lie in the areas of concrete for the footings and lengths of framing timbers, plus a small amount of roofing materials. The cost of these extra materials is not a significant factor. You will save in the long run by adding the extra 2 feet.

Footings

In many areas you must have footings for garages and other outbuildings just as you do for houses. Consider digging footings for all four sides, even though you will not likely enclose the final wall. If you decide to convert the shelter to a room in the future, you will need the footings.

Dig the footings deep enough that they are below the frost line. Even in areas where there are no frosts, dig below the topsoil until you reach the hard, firmly packed clay. Footings should be 18–24 inches wide. If you are digging your own footings, do so, if possible, after a long and slow rain so the soil will be very soft down to a depth of several inches. Digging in baked soil in August can be a very exhausting and slow process.

Many contractors simply pour concrete into the footings. Some old-time builders insist on a bed of sand, then 3 or 4 inches of gravel before the concrete is poured. The theory is that the bed of sand will keep the footings from sinking or settling even a fraction of an inch. You can keep in mind that a bed of concrete is also unlikely to settle appreciably.

If you mix and pour your own concrete, you will appreciate the fact that you kept the banks of the footings straight and even. If you allow them to slope outward you will need far more concrete.

Before making the decision about concrete, take into consideration your time, the cost of the mix, as well as the costs of sand, gravel, the mortar box, and implements—if you must buy them. You will pay $20–$25 per day to rent a mixer, the concrete mix will cost you at least $40, and the sand and gravel will cost a total of at least $40. You will have at least $100 tied up in footings, when you can probably have them poured for $200 or slightly less in many parts of the country.

Lay off the footing lines, and after the footings trenches are dug, level the footings. You can do this without a transit or other sophisticated equipment by driving a stake into the bottom of the footing so that the top of it is equal to the desired depth of the concrete. Check with your local building inspector to learn how deep the concrete in a footing must be.

When you have driven in the stake, select a timber with a straight and true edge. Move the length of the timber away from the first stake and drive in another. Lay the timber on top of the two stakes, then lay a level on top of the timber. If the level reading shows that the tops of the two stakes are even, you can move on to the third stake. Level it with the second, and in this manner proceed all the way around the footings. When you come to the final stake, lay the timber on top of the last and also on top of the first one. The two should have a level reading.

You are now ready to pour the concrete. When you pour it, smooth it as you work and make sure that the concrete is even with the tops of the stakes. If all the stakes have concrete to the very top, you know that your footings are level. If you spot any obviously high spots between stakes, smooth these by pushing the concrete to the lower areas. If you must, shovel out some of the concrete rather than have some areas higher than you need them.

Remove the stakes and smooth over the concrete where it was disturbed. Smooth the entire footings area. Allow the footings to set for at least 24 hours before you begin framing work. Some contractors will lay blocks or bricks on concrete that has just been poured, but good building practices dictate waiting until there is a solid foundation in the footings trenches.

Foundation wall

The next task is to build a foundation wall, if you plan to have one. For the typical carport you can build a wall of cement blocks 2 feet high, or you can face the wall with bricks.

Lay your sills out on top of the wall and mark them for cutting. You can use anchor bolts to secure the sills to the foundation walls if you wish. These bolts cost less than 50 cents each, and they strengthen the building considerably. Bolts should be installed every 2 or 4 feet.

The sills should be treated lumber wide enough to cover the top of the foundation wall completely. Do not leave concrete blocks open so that rain and insects can find their way in. Many spiders, mice and other rodents, and small snakes find these areas to be ideal for their uses.

If you choose to build directly on top of the footings, use termite shields, which are thin strips of metal under wood to prevent termites from finding their way into the wood area of a building. You will not want to build with wood directly over concrete—particularly if the concrete stays moist—unless you use specially treated wood that protects against insect infestation and decay.

Wall assemblies

You can now construct your wall assemblies on the ground and raise them into place, unless you are working alone and the foundation wall is too high to permit such work. Use 4-×-4 timbers for corner posts, or two 2 × 4s firmly fastened together.

Lay out the walls by marking the sole plate and top plate for stud location. Keep all studding spaced 16 inches on center. For the corner posts use the best, straightest, and best-looking timbers. Nail in the studding and frame for rough window openings.

When you raise the wall assembly, nail brace timbers to the wall assembly and run these timbers to a stake driven firmly into the ground nearby. Nail the brace to the stake. Do this on two sides until you are ready to tie walls together.

If you are building on top of a foundation wall, you will need to install the sole plate, stand your corner posts in place and attach them to the sill, then establish your brace timbers to hold the corner post in place. Move to the other end of the wall and repeat the process. Keeping the brace timbers in place, install the top plate and nail it to the top of the corner posts. At this point you have a large rectangle.

Now cut and install the studding. Rather than assembling a wall on the ground and raising it, you are building the wall in place because of the difficulty in lifting the assembled wall to the top of the foundation wall.

If you are building a garage or carport where a full concrete floor has been poured, you can assemble the walls on the floor and then lift them into place. The floor serves the same here as subflooring does in the typical house.

When the corner posts of the wall are in place, cut and add the studding. Move to the wall that joins the one just framed and repeat the process Keep both walls braced well on two sides. Nail the corner posts together securely so that the two walls are tied together at one corner. You can also nail a short length of 2 × 4 across the top of the angle formed by the two walls. You will remove this brace piece later, so do not drive the nails in all the way.

When the third wall is formed, tie the corner posts together by driving in several nails along the length of the two walls. You can brace the wall and also nail in the short timber across the corner.

The fourth wall will not be studded or framed for a carport. You can run the top plate across the span from the two side walls. One practice is to run two timbers across the front and install cripple studs with 16-inch centers between the two timbers, which are about 1 foot apart (FIG. 10-1).

10-1 Provide extra strength to the garage opening by constructing a miniature wall, with header timbers substituting for sole plate and top plate, and with short "studs" between the two header timber assemblies.

When you add the top capping you tie the walls together even better, and bridging and bracing will strengthen each individual wall. When the walls are completed, install ceiling joists. These will also greatly strengthen the structure. Install these joists as you would studding, with

16-inch center spacing. Add bridging between the joists for greater stability.

This process will easily serve for a typical carport. If you want a double carport, frame and erect the three basic walls, and before you add the timbers to tie the front wall to the framing, frame a fourth wall that divides the two bays of the carport. The top capping of the middle wall frame serves as a girder, and when you install joists, notch them and let them meet at the center of the top cap. Install a joist for every stud in the side walls.

When this is done, add the tie-in timbers across the front wall, let the joists serve as the tie-ins. You are now ready to frame the roof.

A CARPORT ROOF

Remember that the formula for determining the length of a rafter is that for finding the length of the long side of a triangle. After you have decided on the height of the roof, square that number. If the roof is to be 5 feet higher than the joists, that number squared will be 25. Decide on the amount of eaves or overhang you will want, and measure from the center of the girder to the end of the joists. If you want a 1-foot eave, add that number to the total. If the distance from the center of the girder to the end of the eaves is 13 feet, square that number. The figure is 169. Now add the two squared figures: 25 plus 169. The result is 194. You now need to figure the square root of 194. The square root of 194 is 13.928 or 13.9. The length of the rafters will then be 13 feet, 11+ inches. For easier calculation, make the rafters 14 feet long.

Decide the overhang on the front and back of the carport. If you decide upon 1 foot in each place, add 2 feet to the length of the carport. That is the length of the ridge board you will need to install.

Slant cut the ends of the rafters. (See Chapter 5 for the best means of determining the angle of the slant cut.) Nail one end of a rafter to the ridgeboard, which is already atop the carport framing. Go to the other side of the ridgeboard and add a second rafter. You are now ready to lift the ridgeboard and nail the rafter ends in place over the wall framing. Nail the rafter beside the joist and over the stud.

When rafters are nailed in place, go down the ridgeboard and install the remaining rafters. Continue until all rafters are in place. Be sure to include the final rafter that will frame the overhang or eaves (FIG. 10-2).

Use an abundance of bridging to help support the overhang rafter. Install the first piece at the end of the rafter and tie it to the second rafter at the end of the overhang. Every 16 inches add another bridging timber until the rafters are all tied together. You are now ready to install the support for the framing. You can add bridging in addition to the usual supports.

COMPLETING THE FRAME SUPPORTS

Bridging works wonders in strengthening and stabilizing a building frame. Every piece of siding or roof sheathing will add to the stability of

10-2 When constructing the roof line of a gable roof, use a ridgeboard and all of the necessary supports and allow for an overhang or eaves in the front and in the back, as well as on both sides.

the building. If you have not added the bracing and bridging to the joists, now is a good time to install these very necessary timbers.

You can buy thin steel bridging. These strips are nailed to the top and bottom of each joist and serve to keep the joists from leaning or giving in any direction. If you choose to use the steel bridging, you will be able to buy a box of 100 for about $25 or slightly more.

You can also cut and install your own bridging. Measure the distance between the joists and cut the bridging segments from 2-× 6 stock. Cut along the line exactly so that you will have a perfect fit for the bridging. Install bridging pieces by driving nails through the opposite side of the joist and into the end of the bridging. Do this on both sides. Drive one nail about 1 inch from the upper edge, a second nail at the midpoint, and a third 1 inch from the bottom edge.

If you have trouble with nails missing the bridging, use your level or other straightedge to mark along the joist from top to bottom. Keep the line vertical so the bridging will be installed in an upright fashion. Tap the bridging piece until the line is even with the center of the bridging material. Then drive nails along the line and you will be assured of having a good seat for the nails. You can do the same with the ceiling joists. One effective method is to use metal strip bridging in the center of the joists and use wood bridging at each end.

You can also buy joist supports, hangers, or holders. These cost about 75 cents each. They can be fitted over the bottom of the joist so that the sides extend upward and spread along the girder so it can be nailed in place easily and quickly. These holders or supports will keep the joists level and prevent any settling or sinking because of soft wood or other similar problems.

When rafters are installed you can install bridging or supports between the rafters. Install these as you would regular joist bridging.

One alternative is to order preconstructed trusses for the rafters. You can have the trusses made to order by telling the dealer exactly how wide your structure is and how much overhang you want. These trusses cost about $50 each, so if you are buying them for a house or large garage or carport, the cost can run into the hundreds of dollars. When you order, ask if the cost includes setting the trusses upon the top caps or plates for you. Some dealers include this service in their costs, and all you need to do is free one truss and slide it along the plates to the other end of the framework. Nail the truss in place and then slide the next one into position.

This work usually requires at least two men. If the cost of trusses does not include setting them on top of the framing, you will need a crew of at least five men. Alternatively, you could pay someone with a boom truck to set the trusses up for you.

Keep in mind that if you order trusses for a house that is 52 feet long, the cost of the trusses will be about $1300. You will then have to buy bracing, sheathing, and shingles. The total cost of your roof can exceed $2000 very easily. If you buy the lumber and frame your own roof, you will spend extra hours working but you can save at least $800 on the trusses. It ultimately becomes a question of whether your time and effort are worth more than your money.

If you build your own trusses, when the ridgeboard is installed and the rafters are nailed in place, you can install a W bracing, in addition to the regular ties discussed in Chapter 4. This bracing consists of diagonal braces installed so that they vaguely resemble the letter W, with a girder serving as the middle of the letter.

STORAGE OR APARTMENT ROOM

Depending upon the height of the ridgeboard and the width of the carport or garage, you might have room to frame in a small apartment or sleeping quarters for guests. Such an apartment will be very hot in summer and cold in winter unless good weather preparations are made. These include a small air conditioning unit and a small heating system.

The apartment will have a very low ceiling and even lower walls at each extreme of the rooms. Before starting to work, measure the height of the bottom of the ridgeboard. There will need to be at least 7 feet of head room in the center.

Measure from the top of the subflooring to the rafters near the outside of the attic space. You will need at least 4 feet of space if you plan to use the area for storage or sleeping. If you decide that you have enough room for a small apartment, install a sole plate where you plan to have the wall on each side of the attic. Studs can be nailed from the sole plate to the rafters.

Hold the studs in place beside the rafter and mark where the rafter crosses the stud. Cut along the line and when you install the stud, position it so that the slant cut fits under the rafter. Nail the stud in place by driving nails through the slant cut and into the rafter. Do this on all rafters.

When all studding is in place, nail up wall coverings, such as plywood. If you use very thin wall coverings like paneling, you will need to install lath or nailing boards horizontally at the bottom, top, and middle of the studs.

You can nail in plywood or Sheetrock on the underside of the rafters to form a slanted ceiling. The Sheetrock or plywood will meet at the peak of the framing. You can install molding there later to cover the juncture. Do the same at the point where the walls meet the ceiling.

Because of the low ceiling, the area near the walls will need to be used for sleeping or for storage or placement of low items of furniture. Refrigerators and other high units of furniture will have to be placed along the end walls or near the center of the room.

You can finish the rooms by installing finished wall coverings, flooring, and lighting. You will want to wire and plumb the rooms while they are still in the framing stages.

Unless you have an unusually large garage or carport, your rooms will be not much larger than 20 feet long and 16 feet wide, and of this space only the center part of the room can be used for traffic. Despite the smallness of the quarters, the rooms can be rented to students or, as indicated earlier, used as temporary quarters for guests.

Access to the rooms will be either by inside stairs or outside stairs or steps. Because of limited space inside, many people prefer an outside set of steps with a small covered landing at the top. The entry door is also located at the landing, which is often on the back side of the garage; otherwise the steps would interfere with the use of the garage bays.

Chapter ▌▌

Adding porches or decks

*I*n recent decades there has been a growing popularity of decks and a corresponding receding popularity of porches, particularly front porches. There are a few reasons for the diminishing popularity of front porches. Many years ago streets were quiet and shady. Homeowners liked to sit on the porch in the late afternoon or evening and enjoy the cool air. The porch often served as a social gathering place for neighbors to congregate.

Today streets are paved, and the heat retained by the pavement negates the coolness of the evening air. The increasing number of automobiles causes noise and air pollution. Because of television, fewer people seek front porch entertainment. Air conditioning makes homes cooler and more desirable than porches. At the same time, the need for a social gathering place remained a part of Americana as business associates, families, and special interest groups moved to the back of the house. The deck has become a favorite place for cookouts and small parties.

Many people reasoned that the front porch is now too expensive for the limited use it provides. It costs as much to roof and floor the porch as it does to roof and floor the same amount of space inside the house, and yet is used far less. Many people feel that even if the porch was closed in and converted to a room, the long, narrow dimensions would not produce a room suitable for a bedroom or family room.

You might want to reconsider this trend, particularly with reference to the back or side porch. A porch that is 12 feet wide and 32 feet long, or even 52 feet long, can be converted—if the need arises—to a series of rooms 12 feet wide and 13 feet long. You could actually have four such rooms from one long porch, or three rooms that are slightly larger than 12 × 10, or two rooms that are 12 by 16. Remember that in many modern homes the bedrooms are only 12 by 10 or slightly larger. Many are even smaller.

If you are undecided about ever requiring more rooms, you might decide to build a deck or porch to use for social occasions with the understanding that it can be converted into rooms later on. Start by selecting a size. If you decide on a deck that is 8 feet wide, remember that you will not be able to convert the deck into a room, unless you choose to make it into a bathroom, a utility room, or storage space or pantry. If you make the deck or porch 10 to 12 feet wide, the space can later serve as a bedroom. Once you make the decision, you can stake off the footings and begin work.

Dig footings with a spade and mattock if they do not have lengthy dimensions. Some decks are installed with posts in holes serving as the supports. If you choose to use this approach, you will not need the footings. After the footings are dug and poured and leveled at all points, you are ready to build either the foundation wall (for a porch) or set the piers or supports (for a deck). Both tasks are equally important and should be carried out with careful attention.

BUILDING A DECK

Use treated timbers for all decking lumber. Even the rails should be treated. A deck will receive a significant amount of precipitation, and the droplets of moisture standing on or clinging to the wood will eventually soak into the wood. This renders the wood susceptible to insect damage because the moisture is an invitation to a wide variety of insects, including termites.

Support Posts

Set the pier supports either in holes, using special creosoted or similarly treated posts that will resist decay, or on top of the footings. Footings will be used only for above-ground installation. If you are using in-ground posts, dig the holes adequately deep. Also, erect the posts carefully to keep them level and also to stabilize them completely. Stabilize posts by first setting them in the holes, then packing dirt loosely around them. Finally, mix a bag of mortar mix with water until you have a very loose or plastic mixture and pour the mixture into the hole. If the mixture is loose enough that it can permeate the soil, the dirt will become the aggregate and you will have a very sturdy post.

If you set the posts atop footings, you will need to use a lot of bracing timbers to keep the posts vertical as you work. Start by nailing one end of a long brace timber (10 feet or so) to the post about 5 feet off the ground. Use only one nail so that timber can move freely. When the post is erect and the brace timber is supporting it partially, drive a stake beside the lower end of the brace timber and nail the timber to the stake.

Nail another brace timber to the post at about the same height as the first one. This second timber should be installed at a 90-degree angle to the first. If one timber is pointing north, the other should be pointing east or west. Drive another stake and nail the free end of the second timber to this stake.

In both instances drive the nail in only far enough to hold the support timber in place. If you are working alone, you will need to make minor adjustments to level the post, so move the end of the brace timber in or out as you work.

The post is now supported sufficiently for you to position it in a perfectly vertical manner. Use a level to check for accurate setting. If you need to make adjustments, free the stake end of the timber and move it in or out as needed. Rest the end of the timber securely on the ground while you stop to check the level reading of the post. If you have a helper, one of you can read the level while the other makes the necessary adjustments.

When the reading is satisfactory, nail the end of the support timber to the stake again and make the same changes, if necessary, at the other stake. When you are satisfied that the post is positioned accurately, add another nail or so to hold the support timbers securely in place.

In every case, check the corners for squareness before you leave the posts. When all of them are set properly, you are ready to install the basic framing timbers.

Framing Timbers

Treat the framing timbers as if you were framing a house. The major difference at this point is that you are working without a foundation wall.

Use bolts rather than nails when you are framing. A nail will sometimes work its way loose, no matter how well it was nailed. If the wood is cured insufficiently, the tendency of the nails to work free is increased. A bolt will not work free. Even if it loosens, you will be able to tighten the nuts later. You will need to drill a hole through the post as you attach each framing timber. When the timber is in place, tap the bolt through the timber and post, then add a washer and nut on the end that extends through the post.

If for some reason you cannot use bolts and must use spikes (long nails), drill the hole slightly smaller than the shank of the spike, then drive the spike through both framing timber and post. You will need to drill holes because the length of the spike, plus the force needed to drive it, will cause the shank to bend. If the spikes are $3/8$ inch in shank size, use a $1/4$-inch drill bit for the hole. Use a 3-pound hammer to drive the spikes.

Attach the outside framing timbers securely to the posts. Use 2-×-8 or 2-×-10 timbers for the basic framing of the floor. Install these with 16-inch centers. The outside framing timbers will be attached to the outside of the posts so that the ends of the timbers are flush. Abut the ends as you would headers or joists in a house frame.

Joists

When the outside framing is completed, install the joists. Do not simply nail joists into the headers. Use a hanging joist type of installation or use a ledger plate. Use both for added support (FIG. 11-1).

The hanging joist is notched so that one end of it hangs over the top

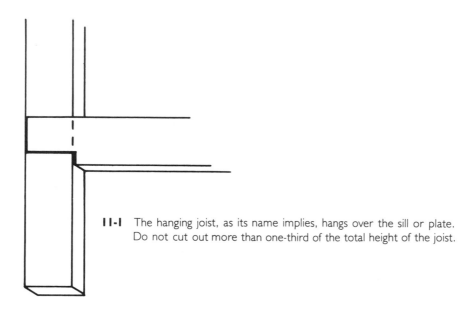

11-1   The hanging joist, as its name implies, hangs over the sill or plate. Do not cut out more than one-third of the total height of the joist.

edge of the framing timber. Do not notch more than one-third of the joist or it will weaken severely. The ledger plate is a 2-×-2 strip of wood that is installed under the bottom edge of the joists. The joists, in addition to being nailed to the headers or framing timbers, are also supported by the ledger strip (FIG. 11-2).

When joists are installed, you are ready to install the flooring. Again, use treated lumber. You can buy $5/4$-inch decking, which is actually $1^1/4$ inches thick nominally. If your joists are on 16-inch centers, this decking will offer good support. If your joists run north-to-south, the decking should run east-to-west.

The railing can now be installed. Use bolts to fasten the rail posts to the framing, then use nails to attach the rails to the posts. Use treated lumber for rails and railing posts.

The dimensions of the deck will determine the length and size of your joists in some cases. Many building codes require that you use a 2-×-10 joist if you have a span of 16 feet. If the span is greater than 16 feet, you will need larger timbers or you will need to add more support posts

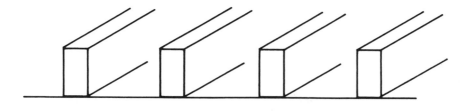

11-2   The ledger plate is often a 2-×-2 timber that is nailed under the joists and snugly against the bottoms of the joists.

to the framing. You should also add bridging between the joists to hold them stable and in an upright position.

You can use metal strip bridging or you can use short lengths of timber cut to fit snugly between the joists. If you use the metal strips, start by placing one strip so that the end is atop the first joist or header. Drive a nail through the hole in the strip and bend the strip downward so that the other end will fit under the next joist. Move to the bottom of the first joist and place another bridging strip so that the end is across the bottom of the joist. Nail it as you did before and bend this strip upward so that the other end will rest on the top of the second joist.

Before you nail the strips on the second joist, place the third strip so that the hole in it is aligned with the hole in the second strip on top of the second joist. Nail the two strips in place at the second time. Do the same with the strip on the bottom of the second joist. Maintain this pattern all the way across the deck joist system. When you are finished you will have an X between any two joists. By nailing the strips in the pattern described you will keep the joists from moving out of vertical alignment. Neither the top nor the bottom of the joist can move more than a fraction of an inch. In this simple manner you have strengthened your joist framing immensely.

You can also buy joist holders that fit over the bottom end of the joists and have flared sides with holes so that you can nail the holders to the girder or header. Check with your local building code to see if these holders are suggested or required. They can be bought for less than $1 each.

Building a deck, like framing a room, is a project where you can cut corners in several places. Some of these cost cutting moves are good, while others are very dangerous or far more costly in the long run. Do not ever try to economize at the risk of safety or at the chance of failing an inspection. If the deck does not meet basic safety standards, the money you saved will be a classic example of false economy.

FRAMING A PORCH

You will find that framing a porch is similar to framing a deck or room. The basics are the same in most cases: you need footings, headers, joists, ledger plates, and in this case you also need a foundation wall for best results.

Start, if you are adding a porch to an existing house, by measuring and laying off the porch area. Take care to square the corners and establish a true reading on all sides of the porch. Stake off the porch area just as you would for a house. Mark the footing lines by using flour, sand, fertilizer, or any other powdery or grainy substance that will stand out in contrast to the soil.

Even though you are not planning to use the porch as a part of the living area of the house, building code standards still are in effect. You must secure a building permit in most instances. The typical building code requires that you secure a permit for any type of work that alters the outside shape or silhouette of your house. You should realize that this ruling is a good one generally, because the same law that keeps you from adding a porch without permission also keeps your neighbors from erecting eyesores and dangerous buildings adjacent to your property.

Footings

You must, in most cases, dig and pour footings because there is the possibility that in the future the next owner of the house will decide to close in the porch and create extra bedrooms for the house. Keep in mind that any room that has a full closet can be considered a bedroom in the eyes of the building and health inspectors, and any part of the house that has a permanent floor and roof may be interpreted as a future room. Such rooms must meet all the code requirements.

Foundation walls and piers

When footings are poured (see Chapter 2), you are ready to build your foundation wall and piers, if any. Remember that you need a pier for any long unsupported runs of framing timbers. Some runs can be spanned by a 2 × 6, while others require a 2 × 8, 2 × 10, or even a 2 × 12, depending upon the length of the span.

If you do not choose to buy the timbers heavy enough to have a prolonged span, build piers by digging a square hole deep enough to pass the frost or freeze line and to pass the topsoil that is likely to sink and give with the weight of the porch. One of the best ways to build a pier is to fill in the bottom of the hole with 2 or 3 inches of sand and then add 3 or 4 inches of gravel. On top of the gravel pour concrete, and on top of the concrete build a pier of either bricks or concrete blocks and mortar these together with a proper bonding arrangement.

You will find that in many cases the piers consist only of blocks or bricks stacked and fitted securely under the joists. Your building code may permit such a structure, but keep in mind that the building code specifies only the lowest or minimum acceptable level. You will spend a little more time and effort if you build the piers properly, but the finished results will be far more satisfactory.

After the foundation wall is laid, you can start to frame the porch. Start with sills. These wide timbers should be of treated lumber. Rain often blows in on a porch and the water seeps through cracks and rots the sills. Treated sills are resistant to decay and insect infestation.

Lay the sills flat over the foundation wall top. Install termite shields at this time if you plan to use them. A termite shield is a thin, flat strip of metal that is placed between the sill and the foundation wall. The strip extends over the edge of the foundation wall and keeps termites from climbing the wall and entering the house. If you cannot locate termite shields in your area, you can buy thin metal and use tin or metal snips to cut your termite shields.

Anchor the sills to the foundation wall by using anchor bolts. These bolts cost less than 50 cents each and come with nuts and washers. Install them by filling the holes in the top courses of blocks with mortar or concrete. While the mortar is still plastic, drill holes in the sills and run the threaded end of the bolt up through the hole from the bottom. Then add the washer and nut. Set the sill on the foundation wall so that the bolts with the angled ends sink into the wet or green mortar. When the mortar sets, the bolts will be firmly secured. Tighten the nuts so that the sills are tight against the foundation wall after the mortar has set fully and has cured for a day or two.

Joists

Install the joists and headers just as you did for the basic house. You can fit two headers or outside timbers together so that the ends fit evenly as one abuts the other. Nail a temporary support strip across the angle formed by the two headers. This support strip will hold the two timbers together. In this fashion you can install the headers or upright joists for the entire porch. Nail the ends together by driving nails through the end of one timber and into the end of the one that abuts it. When this is done, you can install the joists.

Many people like to build the lower part of the foundation wall from 12-inch blocks, then add one final course or row of 8-inch blocks. The joists can then rest on the 4-inch expanse of blocks formed where the 8-inch block sits on the 12-inch block.

If you used blocks all the same size, you can solve the support problem by using joist holders. These metal devices fit under the joist and have flat surfaces flush against the headers so that you can nail them in place. In addition to the joist holders or supports, drive nails through the header from the outside and into the end of the joist. When this is done for all joists, add the bridging.

Subflooring

You are now ready for the subflooring. Run the panels of plywood subflooring at right angles to the joists. By using this arrangement you will have seven joists covered by one panel, for a total of 96 inches of running space. This will be tied together by one panel of the subflooring. Cover the entire porch in this fashion. Be sure to measure by using the on-center spacing so that each panel will reach half of the way across the joist top. Leave space at the top or there will be no way to nail the panel beside the one you just installed.

After the subflooring is in place, you can add the support posts. Some builders suggest using building paper between subflooring and flooring. You might find, as others have, that any water that seeps between the finished flooring will be trapped by the nonporous building paper and held there. The results are rapid decaying and ideal breeding places for insects. If you do add the building paper, it is a good idea to use a water seal application on the porch. These products work well and can be applied in a matter of minutes over a space the size of the typical porch.

Some builders also suggest that you use thick decking and leave tiny cracks between the boards so that water can escape. The problem here is trying to convert the porch into a room, if you decide to do so later on, without having to completely rework the flooring. The water seal application usually solves the problem and leaves you with the later option of enclosing and converting the porch into a room of the house.

You can install the finished flooring of the porch before you install the posts. You can also install the posts over subflooring and use a sole plate—which must be of treated lumber—then abut the finished flooring to the sole plate. It is easier and perhaps more effective to install the posts over the finished flooring. If you use the sole plate with the abutted flooring, there will be a crack that can permit moisture to seep down to the subflooring.

Posts and ceiling framing

One of the basic differences between a deck and a porch is that a porch has a roof, and often a ceiling, while the deck is open. Install porch posts in much the same way you would frame a room, with this difference: The porch has a minimum number of posts rather than a series of 16-inch on-center studs. If you have too many posts, the view is cluttered, so you must decide what size posts to use and how many to use.

Use nothing smaller than a 4-×-4 post. You can space these posts every 2 feet rather than 16 inches, and some builders space them even farther apart than 2 feet. Some codes will allow you to space them as much as 5 feet apart. You can also, within some codes, use two 2 × 4s nailed together instead of one 4 × 4.

The suggestion here is to use only 4 × 4s and to space them no more than 4 feet apart. Set them on the finished flooring. Start at one corner and use two brace timbers to hold the post in a temporary position until you can nail it in place. Then install the second post in the same way. Toe-nail the bottom of the post to the flooring.

When all the posts in one wall are temporarily installed, nail a plate over the tops to tie them together. Erect the posts on the adjacent wall and tie these to the first wall. Keep temporary bracing intact until the porch posts are fully tied together.

When the basic framing is complete, install the ceiling joists from the house to the outside edge of the framing. Use necessary bridging between ceiling joists. Keep the porch framing as sturdy and secure as you can get it. The bridging will strengthen the porch considerably in terms of sturdiness (FIG. 11-3).

The porch posts that are spaced 4 feet apart are such that later, if you decide to enclose the porch, you can add studs between posts and you will have the basic 16-inch on-center framing intervals. Start at the corner post and measure over 16 inches and install the stud. Then move to the 32-inch point and install a second stud. Do this between posts and your room will be ready to cover with sheathing or similar materials.

You can also add ceiling joists on the same 16-inch spacing and use the ceiling for the porch, or it can later be used for the ceiling of a room.

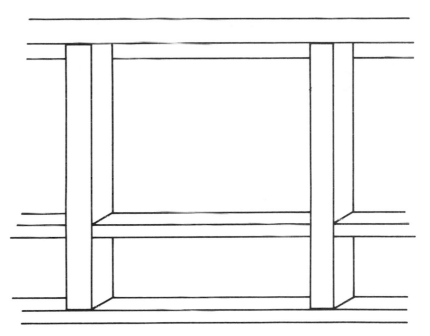

II-3 When installing porch posts, use nothing smaller than a 4 × 4. Add strength and stability by adding a length of timber between posts at the top and bottom.

It is a good idea to plan the porch as if it will definitely become a part of your residential area at a later date, unless the porch is so small that it could not possibly be used.

When the ceiling is framed, install rafters from the edge of the porch—allowing for a 2-foot overhang—to the house wall just under the eaves of the existing roof. In this way all rain that runs off the existing roof will fall onto the porch roof and then be diverted off the overhang or into guttering. You can slant-cut the ends of porch rafters and fit them onto the existing roof lines. Add bridging and other supports and then sheath the roof as you did the roof of the house.

Use plywood for the most rapid covering of the porch roof. You can use board sheathing, but the work is slow and the cost is rather high. You can cover 32 square feet with one panel of plywood in a matter of 5 to 10 minutes. If you use board sheathing, you will need about 10 5-inch sheathing boards 8 feet long in order to cover the same amount of space. You will also need to drive about 140 nails, while with plywood you will need to drive only about 30 for one panel.

The cost of plywood is also much less than that of board sheathing. One advantage of board sheathing is that you will not have all boards ending at the same rafter or joist, while with plywood you usually have several panels ending on the same rafter.

Be sure to install braces and supports under the roof rafters and nail these to both rafters and joists. You can slant-cut the ends of the support timbers so that they will fit under the rafters rather than being nailed against them. Supports that are nailed to the sides of rafters are not as satisfactory as those installed under the rafters.

You are now ready to shingle the roof. At this point the porch is finished, as far as rough carpentry is concerned. You will later need to add the finish flooring, ceiling, roofing, and the final enclosing timbers.

Glossary

anchor bolt a bolt, usually 8 inches long or longer, with a curve or angle on one end and threads on the other end. The anchor bolt is usually installed through the sill and embedded in mortar or concrete inside the blocks in a foundation or basement wall.

bird's-mouth cut a notch at the outside end of a rafter that permits it to fit snugly and evenly against the top plate of a wall frame.

brace and bit a tool, usually hand-operated, that is used to bore or drill holes in wood. It is similar to the electric drill in function and is sometimes called an auger.

boxing boards or plywood used to enclose the rafters and eaves.

bracing any type of reinforcement that serves to keep a part of a structure steady and strong. Let-in bracing is installed between studding, while cut-in bracing is actually installed in slits or notches made in the edge of a stud or other timber.

bridging a type of bracing used between joists or rafters to keep them from turning and warping. The bridging, which may be metal or wood, keeps the joists or rafters the same distance apart.

cap, top a 2 × 4 or similar timber over the top plate in a wall frame.

carriage a part of a stairway that supports the treads.

cleat a small strip of wood nailed under the treads of a stairway to help support the treads. Cleats are used generally when the stringers are not cut out to hold the treads.

clinching sinking a nail firmly into the wood so that the head is embedded in the wood so tightly that it will not pull loose.

collar ties timbers nailed or bolted to rafters slightly below the ridgeboard or ridge pole. These ties support the rafters and keep them from spreading.

cross bridging bracing that is installed in the form of a wide × for the purpose of strengthening and solidifying joists or rafters.

dormers a roof structure that projects outward, forming a vertical wall and space for a window.

drywall gypsum rock made into paper-covered panels, 4 × 8 or 4 × 12 feet, used for wall covering. Sheetrock, plasterboard, or gypsum board.

eaves the overhang of a roof line.

footings trenches dug below the frost line around the wall lines of a house or other structure, then filled with concrete to provide support for foundation walls and the weight of the house.

gable any structurally planned roof angle that creates a roof peak on any part of the roof line.

girder heavy timber or other support piece that runs the length of a building. Girders support the rafter system and roof and tie the walls together.

gusset bracing plywood or similar materials that are fitted to and nailed against the junctures formed by rafters and ridgeboard or rafters and joists.

gypsum board see drywall.

header a perimeter timber where joists or other framing timbers are installed.

horses the stringers of a stairway.

jacks, hip part of the rafter system of a hip roof.

joist a long timber that helps support the floor of a structure. The subflooring is usually nailed on top of the joists.

lath a strip of wood or similar material that is used as a nailer for plywood, paneling, or other wall coverings.

ledger plate a length of lumber, usually 2 inches wide, nailed against a girder or header and used to support the joists in a wall frame.

load bearing wall any wall in a structure that supports or helps to support the weight of the building above it.

nosing the slight extension of a stairway tread over the riser.

partition wall any wall in a structure that is not load-bearing.

plate the top and bottom timbers in a wall frame. The sole plate is the timber nailed to the subflooring and to which the ends of the studs are nailed. The top plate is nailed to the upper ends of the studding.

plumb cut a saw cut that is perfectly vertical.

rafter a timber that extends from the ridgeboard to the eaves of a roof or from one end or side of a roof line to the other.

rafter, common an ordinary rafter that runs from front to back of a roof line or from ridgeboard to eaves.

ridgeboard a long timber that runs the full length of a roof line and to which all of the rafters are nailed.

riser a board or length of wood installed at the back of a step in a stairway.

rise the height from floor level a rafter or stairway rises from its lowest to highest points.

run the linear distance covered by a roof or stairway.

sheathing any of several types of wall or roof coverings nailed to rafters or studding and to which the finished wall or roof is nailed.

Sheetrock see drywall.

story pole a 2 × 4 or other timber used to measure the height of each course of blocks or bricks so that all courses or units are level.

stringer a long timber, usually one of two or three in a stairway, to which the treads and risers are attached.

stud, common a length of 2 × 4 installed between the top plate and sole plate of a wall frame.

stud, cripple a short stud installed in such locations as between window sills and sole plates.

stud, trimmer a length of 2 × 4 used inside door and window frames.

termite shield a strip of metal installed between foundation walls and sills to prevent termites from entering a structure.

toenailing nailing at an angle.

tongue-and-groove lumber with a furrow on one edge and a ridge on the other, so that the two edges fit snugly when installed in a floor or wall.

treads the steps in a stairway.

trusses assemblies consisting of rafters, braces, and supports.

Index